Stitched

Stitched

A step-by-step guide to
the fashionable world of sewing

ROS BADGER

This edition published by Parragon Books Ltd in 2016

Parragon Inc.
440 Park Avenue South, 13th Floor
New York, NY 10016
www.parragon.com

ISBN 978-1-4748-0421-9

Printed in China

Written by Ros Badger
Projects designed and made by Ros Badger
Edited by Sarah Hoggett
Designed and produced by Sue Pressley and
    Paul Turner, Stonecastle Graphics Ltd
Photography by The Photography Firm on location at
    The Tack Barn, Upper Lodge, Sussex, UK.

NOTES FOR THE READER

This book uses both metric and imperial
measurements. Follow the same units of
measurement throughout; do not mix metric
and imperial. This book is sold subject to the
condition that all designs and instructions
contained in it are copyrighted and not for
commercial reproduction without the permission
of the publisher, Parragon Books Ltd.

To the fullest extent permitted by law, the
author and the publisher: (i) cannot and do not
accept any legal duty of care or responsibility
in relation to the accuracy or appropriateness
of the contents of this book; and (ii) disclaim
any liability, loss, damage, or risk that may be
claimed or incurred as a consequence—directly
or indirectly—of the use and/or attempted
use of any of the contents of this book.

Additional photography

Stonecastle Graphics Ltd: *p47; p57; p58 row 3 left; p65; p70
above right; p75 below left; p76; p79 above; p84; p93; p113;
p116; p119 below.* iStock.com: *p8 row 1 right, row 3 right,
row 4 right; p10 below left; p11 row 1 left, row 1 right, row
2 center, row 3 left, row 3 right, row 4 left; p12 below left;
p14 above left, below right; p16 above right; p21 above; p22
below; p23 above left, below right; p24 below left; p25; p26
above left; p28 below right; p31 row 3 left, row 4 right; p37
row 1 left, row 1 right, row 2 left, row 3 left, row 3 center,
row 3 right, row 4 left, row 4 right.* Shutterstock.com: *p7;
p8 row 1 left, row 3 left; p11 row 2 left, row 3 center, row 4
right; p13 above right; p17 below right; p18 below left; p19;
p26 below right; p31 row 1 left, row 1 center, row 2 center,
row 2 right, row 3 center, row 4 left; p33 below left; p34
below; p37 row 2 center; p38 row 1 left; p53.*

CONTENTS

INTRODUCTION

With so many gorgeous fabrics on the market, from printed cottons and plain linens to luxurious silks and velvets, it's never been easier to create stylish, one-of-a-kind projects—and all you need to get started are a few simple tools and techniques.

I began sewing as a young child, making doll's clothes held together with huge running stitches, the odd safety pin, staples, and occasionally even sticky tape! Those first experiences created a life-long love of the craft: transforming a piece of cloth into something else, whether it's an item of clothing or a stylish piece to brighten up your home, still seems like magic to me.

And it appears that lots of other people feel the same, as more people than ever before are asking me to show them how to sew. So I've put together this guide to simple yet stylish sewing, which I hope you'll use as a starting point for your own creations. It's not a sewing master class, packed with tips and tricks that only professional tailors would attempt; instead, it's a beginners' guide to a few essential techniques to use in combination with a sewing machine, followed by more than 20 projects that you can put your own individual spin on.

If you've never done any sewing before, start by working through the techniques section, which covers both hand and machine techniques that you will use time and time again, practicing on small fabric scraps.

The projects are arranged roughly in order of difficulty—but none of them is particularly taxing, even for complete beginners. Unlike most sewing books, there are no complicated seams or zippers, and the majority of these designs don't require anything more than the ability to sew in a (reasonably!) straight line. I hope that when you finish most of these, you will be confident to start trying more complicated patterns elsewhere. You may even start creating your own!

Feel free to mix and match: if I've used an embroidered motif on an eyeglasses pouch but you'd prefer to put that same motif on a pillow, then do it! If you like the patchwork combination I've used on a quilt but don't want to tackle something that big, scale it down for a handy pencil pouch or makeup bag.

Above all, don't feel constrained to follow my fabric choices. Color and pattern are very much a matter of personal taste, and the fabrics I've used are only suggestions. Some of the projects here use cool, subtle shades and natural, self-colored fabrics like linen, but there's absolutely no reason why the same design wouldn't work just as well in a contemporary print. Equally, you can completely change the look of a project by substituting a plain or small-patterned, vintage-style fabric for a bold, retro pattern.

Take your inspiration for color and pattern combinations from other books and magazines, and things that you see for sale in store. You might even like to make up a scrapbook of color notes and fabric swatches to help you when you go shopping for fabric. (Most fabric stores and online sites are happy to let you order small samples, so you can see the scale of the pattern and feel the weight of the fabric first hand before you buy.)

At a time when most clothes and soft furnishings are mass produced, sewing is not only a way of creating an individual look that you simply can't buy on the high street, but is also a relaxing and rewarding craft. There are few things as satisfying as being able to say, "I made that myself"—and that in itself is reason enough to start stitching. I hope that *Stitched* inspires you to do just that!

Ros Badger

SEWING
BASICS

Sewing is such a rewarding hobby—
and the wonderful thing is that you
really don't need much specialist
knowledge, just an ability to use a
sewing machine, to be able to create
beautiful hand-crafted pieces that
will be the envy of all your friends.
This chapter sets out everything you
need to know, from essential tools
through to buying fabric and working
your very first stitches.

EQUIPMENT

There's a bewildering array of sewing gizmos and gadgets on the market, but you really don't need much to begin with. Start with a few basics, then add extra pieces as and when you need them.

MEASURING AND MARKING TOOLS

The first stage in any sewing project is to measure and mark out the fabric pieces that you need to cut. Accurate measuring is essential and there are a number of tools to help you.

Dressmaker's tape measure

A tape measure is a flexible strip usually marked with inches on one side and centimeters on the other. Buy the best you can afford, as this piece of kit will be in constant use. Plastic tapes are fine, but they can split and melt if they touch a hot iron. So find a printed linen tape if possible.

A second tape is always useful. Buy a retractable one that you can keep in your purse—always useful when you're buying fabric and notions.

A wooden yard or meter stick

A fixed or folding yard or meter stick is very useful when making patterns or scaling up templates, and for offering a solid, straight edge when marking up fabric with tailor's chalk.

Measuring gauge

A metal measuring gauge is used when marking up hems or folds, for making buttonholes, and for a number of other sewing jobs requiring short, flat accurate measurements. Available in a variety of forms, the most common is a 6-inch/15-cm sliding rule most often made from aluminum.

Plastic diamond-shaped gauges are also available, with markings for common sewing measurements such as seam allowances, turned edges, and hem widths. They can also be useful when making alterations and for quilting and patchwork projects.

When it comes to marking out fabric pieces so that you've got a clear line to cut along, or transferring embroidery patterns onto fabric, there are several options. Which one you choose is largely a matter of personal preference, so experiment to see what suits your requirements best. It's also a good idea to test your chosen method on a piece of scrap fabric to see that the marks show up clearly enough and (just as importantly) that they can be erased if necessary.

Chalk-based markers

Dressmaker's chalk is perfect for drawing around your pattern pieces on fabric before you cut them out. It can be bought in the form of wedge-shaped, triangular slabs known as tailor's chalk, and as chalk pencils, which you can sharpen to a point to draw fine lines and make small markings such as pocket and buttonhole positions.

Soluble markers

You can also buy air- and water-soluble fabric marker pens, where the markings fade on exposure to the air or can be washed out. A few words of warning: air-soluble markers are great for projects that you're going to work on straight away, but they're not so good for complicated motifs that you then put away incomplete in your sewing box as, by the time you come back to it, the lines may well have disappeared! And do not iron over marks made with a water-soluble marker before you wash them out, as you may actually fix the lines permanently, which is the very last thing you want to do. Needless to say, don't use water-soluble markers on fabrics that need to be dry cleaned.

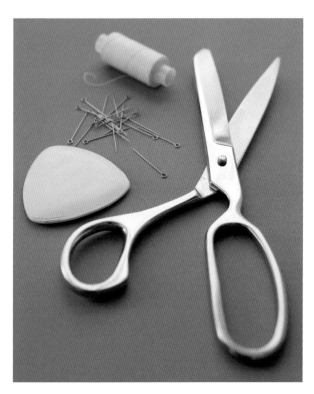

Dressmaker's carbon paper and a tracing wheel

Dressmaker's carbon paper comes in a range of colors. Place it on your fabric, carbon side down, with your pattern or embroidery motif on top. You can either draw over the pattern with a normal pencil, which will leave a solid line on your fabric, or run a tracing wheel (which looks like a mini pizza cutter) over it, which will leave a dotted line on the fabric.

CUTTING TOOLS

A selection of different types of scissors is an essential part of every sewing kit—don't think you can get away with just one pair of multipurpose scissors! You will need at least three different types: paper scissors, dressmaker's shears, and snips or embroidery scissors for cutting thread ends. Most scissors and shears are designed for right-handed people, but left-handed pairs are available from specialist stores. You will also need a seam ripper for rectifying the inevitable sewing mistakes that we all make, such as wonky seams.

Paper scissors

Paper or household scissors (the kind bought in a stationery stores) are used when cutting out templates or paper patterns. Do not use them for cutting fabric or thread, because paper dulls the sharp cutting edge of the blades and they may not cut fabric accurately.

Dressmaker's shears

Dressmaker's shears look very different to standard household scissors. They are longer and have a bent handle that allows the fabric to lie flat on the counter while it is being cut. Shear blades should be around 8 inches/20 cm long or even more. Have them sharpened regularly, and only ever use them for cutting fabric; if you use them to cut paper, they will blunt very quickly. A good pair of shears may seem an expensive investment, but they will last many years.

Embroidery or small sharp scissors

For general sewing, have two pairs of 4-inch/10-cm sharp pointy scissors, also called embroidery scissors, at hand for cutting thread ends after stitching. Keep one pair next to the sewing machine and another pair in your sewing box for handwork. Never, ever cut paper with them, as this will blunt them.

Thread snips

For cutting through sewing and embroidery threads, yarn, and fabric with ease, thread snips are a good alternative to embroidery scissors. Usually around 4 inches/10 cm long, they have no finger holes, but spring together and have very sharp blades.

Seam ripper

All seam rippers are sharp and precise and are used to remove stitching and to cut the slits in buttonholes. Use the blade carefully and the correct way round, as it can easily slip and will rip across the fabric. Remove any loose thread ends before you restitch the seam.

Pinking shears

Pinking shears are not essential, but they are very useful. They have jagged blades fitting together to cut a saw-tooth edge. A pinked edge can be used as a seam finish on tightly woven or nonfraying fabrics. On nonfraying fabric such as fleece, pinking the edges will help reduce a blunt edge showing through when pressing seams. As a decorative edge, it is particularly effective when used on felt.

Rotary cutter

Rotary cutters are mainly used when doing patchwork or quilting as a fast and accurate way to cut small fabric shapes. Use them in conjunction with a self-healing cutting mat—the blade cuts disappear after they are made and the mat provides a nonslip surface.

TIPS

Always cut your thread with sharp scissors, rather than biting it or just snapping it off the reel; this will make it easier to pass through the eye of the needle. Cutting thread at an angle of 45 degrees can also make threading it easier.

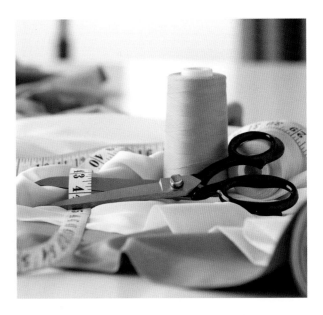

NEEDLES AND PINS

There are lots of different kinds of needle available. Whatever kind you are using, whether you're sewing by hand or by machine, make sure your needles are sharp. Always match your needle size to the fabric that you are using.

Hand sewing needles

A large strong needle and a fine needle are the bare minimum that you will need, but you should really have an assortment of hand sewing needles.

"Sharps" are the most common and useful kind of hand sewing needle. Ranging in size from 1 for coarse fabrics that are difficult to sew to 8 for fine silk, they are of medium length with a round eye and are suitable for most fabrics.

Tapestry and crewel needles are essential items for your sewing kit. Crewel needles have a much longer eye than a sharp and are used for embroidery, while tapestry needles are blunt and are used for canvas work or for hand sewing knitted fabrics.

Specialty hand sewing needles

Used for making furnishings, lampshades, or other household items, specialty needles are available in a wide range, from curved (not for sewing circles!) to flat-edged long steels with a hooklike end.

There are also different types of needle. Regular point needles are used on woven fabrics like cotton and linen; they have a sharp point that penetrates the threads. For knit fabrics such as jersey or fleece, use a ballpoint needle, which has a rounded tip that can pass between the fabric threads.

Twin needles are available for machines with zigzag capability and where the throat plate has a hole wide enough for the double needle. They are perfect for evenly spaced rows of topstitching. If you're going to be sewing lots of heavy fabrics like denim, then invest in some jeans needles.

Needle threader

If you find threading your needles difficult, use a needle threader. This handy little device consists of a piece of wire bent into a diamond shape that is passed through the eye of the needle. The thread is then passed through the wire, which is then pulled back through the eye.

Pins

Strong, straight, and rustproof pins are essential. The standard length of a dressmaker's pin is usually 1 inch/2.5 cm, although shorter pins, which are ½ inch/1.2 cm long, are very useful too, especially on fine fabrics.

The best alternative to flat-headed pins are those with glass or bead heads. These are well worth buying, because they are easy to pick up and they show up well while in use. Usually longer than normal pins at 1 3/8 inch/34 mm in length, they are particularly useful on thick or jersey fabrics.

Safety pins are a handy addition, with a multitude of uses from fixing paper pattern pieces to fabric to threading ties through channels.

Machine needles

Using the wrong size or type of machine needle will cause havoc with any sewing project, producing irregular stitches and causing the thread to snap. At worst, it can result in puckered seams and the piercing of unnecessary holes in your fabric; it can even damage the bobbin, so always be sure to have a good selection of needles so you have the correct size to hand.

Machine needles come in different sizes. The lower the number, the finer the needle—so a size 60/8 is fine for delicate fabrics like silk, while a 100/16 would be suitable for heavy cotton or linen.

TIPS
Always keep hand sewing needles in a case or stick them in a small pincushion—one that the needle can't get lost in amid the stuffing.

SEWING MACHINE NEEDLE GAUGE

Needle size	Fabric weight	Needle type	Fabrics
8–11		Regular point	Chiffon, organza voile
10 or 12	Sheer or fine knit	Ballpoint	Jersey
11		Regular point	Silk, taffeta, tana lawn cotton, chambray fine linen
14	Medium weight	Regular point	Corduroy, linen, velvet, wool, tweed, light ticking, cotton poplin, felt toweling
14	Medium to heavyweight knitted fabric	Ballpoint	Sweatshirt, double knit
16–18	Medium to heavyweight	Regular point	Thick wool, fake fur damask, gabardine, heavy ticking
16	Denim canvas	Denim	Denim and canvas
14 or 16	Specialty heavy	Leather	Leather

OTHER ESSENTIALS

The following bits of kit will all make your sewing life much easier!

Iron and ironing board

A steam iron and ironing board are an essential part of your sewing kit. Most sewing projects include a lot of pressing to produce a professional-looking result and this is impossible to achieve without a good iron, preferably one with strong steam coming from a ceramic foot plate that has plenty of holes, allowing the steam to properly penetrate the fabric.

Other useful but nonessential ironing equipment includes a sleeve roll—a tightly packed, curved form like a hard pillow that makes it easy to press a sleeve or similar tubular piece without leaving creases elsewhere in the fabric. Sleeve rolls also work well when pressing seams open on small projects.

Pincushion

A large pincushion is hugely convenient for holding pins and needles while working and also for storing the needle of the moment. Never keep your needles in the pincushion long term, in case they become lost in the filling. The tighter it is stuffed the better; there are a variety of fillings, from natural fiber stuffings to bran, sawdust, or crushed walnut shells. A wrist or bracelet pincushion can be very useful especially when cutting out, as it's always at hand but not in the way. Simply make a small round pincushion on a cardstock base circle and attach it to an elastic bracelet.

Needle cases

Always put your sewing needles away in a needle case after use and take care to pick them up immediately if you drop them on the floor to avoid accidents.

A fabric book-style case is best; failing that, attach needles to a piece of fabric dedicated to this purpose and keep it away from children. Ideally, make a few cases to keep different sizes and types of needles together. Larger needles like crewel and tapestry needles are best kept in a small tin or tube.

Thimble

A thimble is a small fingertip protector made of metal with a pitted surface that is worn on the finger that pushes the needle into the fabric. Be sure to buy a closed-top dressmaker's style and not a rubber one used for page turning! Thimbles with an opening at the end are used by tailors, as this allows them to manipulate the cloth more easily.

BASIC SEWING KIT

Essentials

Dressmaker's tape measure

A wooden yard or meter stick

Measuring gauge

Tailor's chalk or other fabric marker

Scissors

    Paper scissors

    Dressmaker's shears

    Embroidery scissors or small sharp scissors

    Seam ripper

Straight pins

Safety pins

Pincushion

Magnet or magnetic pin holder for picking up pins
you drop on the floor

Needle case(s)

Thimble

Hand sewing and embroidery needles in a variety
of sizes, including a darning needle

Needle threader

Steam iron and ironing board

Sewing machine with standard and zipper feet

Sewing machine needles in a variety of sizes
and points

Spare bobbins for your sewing machine

Useful extras

Pinking shears

Rotary cutter and self-healing cutting mat

Tweezers—handy when removing thread ends
from a seam that is being undone

TIP

Cotton thread is widely available and ideal for most basic sewing projects, but it is not suitable for stretchy fabrics as it has no "give" and is likely to break when stretched.

SEWING THREADS

Your choice of thread depends on the sewing that is being undertaken. Most basic sewing projects will require no more than a standard cotton or polyester. Match the size and weight of thread to the fabric you are using (you wouldn't choose a delicate cotton thread to sew a heavy-weight denim, for example).

Choose the closest color available to match the fabric—so always buy the thread at the same time as the fabric and be sure to purchase enough! If the exact same color isn't available, choose a darker-toned thread rather than a lighter one. If you're using a printed fabric, choose a thread that matches the main color.

Good-quality thread is worth the money and will make the sewing process easier, too. Thread that is weak will result in a project looking shoddy, as it will break midsewing and show up as stops and starts throughout—or worse, the seams will split when a garment is being worn.

Cotton thread, sold on reels, is ideal for basic sewing. Most brands are mercerized, which gives the thread a lustrous appearance and makes it easily workable.

All-purpose cotton is of a medium thickness and suitable for sewing a wide range of fabrics from lightweight to medium cotton, linen, and rayon and is perfect for delicate fabrics, too.

Polyester threads are stronger than cotton and come in an all-purpose weight, too, with a silicone finish to avoid friction between the thread and fabric when sewing.

Suitable for most machine and hand sewing projects, polyester thread also works better than cotton with stretch fabrics, woven synthetics, and knits. This is because the thread has some give to it, so it won't break when you are working with stretchy knits.

Topstitching thread is thicker in weight than the above and can be threaded as the top thread on a sewing machine to make a more pronounced stitch line. (Use a normal cotton or polyester thread in the bobbin.)

Specialist heavy-duty threads are designed for use on thicker fabrics such as furnishing linens, wool, or woven tweeds.

Clear thread can be useful and is worth having in a sewing box if an invisible line is required on the top of the work.

EMBROIDERY THREADS

With a few simple embroidery stitches, you can transform an everyday item such as a pillow or napkin into something really special and unique. Different kinds of thread create different effects—some have more sheen and sparkle, some have more texture.

Stranded embroidery flosses come in skeins, usually in groups of six strands. They are usually made from cotton, but silk and linen flosses are also available. You can use all six strands together, or untwist the skeins and use fewer strands for a finer embroidery line.

Perle cotton (also known as pearl cotton or coton perlé) is a two-ply embroidery floss with a slight sheen. Like stranded flosses, it is sold in skeins.

Metallic threads can be used for both hand and machine embroidery. They are generally best for adding small hints of sparkle to a design.

CHOOSING FABRICS

Deciding which fabric to use is the most important decision in any sewing project. Your choice allows you to express your individual taste and style and make something that's truly unique.

Always make sure that you read the pattern before you go shopping for fabric, so that you know what kind of fabric and notions you will need. Choosing cloth is exciting, so when you're in the store look around with an open mind. Specialist sales staff are usually very knowledgeable, so ask them questions.

Selecting the correct weave and fiber content is essential; the right color or pattern in the wrong fabric will always be a disaster. When you find a fabric that you like the look of, check its fiber content and make sure that it's suitable for the project you've chosen. Whatever you're making—whether it's a pair of pajamas, a dress for a special occasion, or a pillow cover—the fabric has to marry up with the sewing pattern. It is no use making a sundress in a woolly tweed or a floor pillow from a fine silk.

When handling a fabric, gently rub it between your fingers and thumb. How does it feel? Is it rough or smooth, soft and silky, stiff or brushed, flat or velvety? Ask yourself whether the fabric is suitable for the job— for example, if you're making a summer dress, you may well want a natural fabric that feels comfortable against the skin. Will that color, suit? Is the pattern too big or too small? If it's a small project, a big floral repeat may not be the best choice; conversely, on a large project, a small print may be lost.

When you've made an initial fabric selection, lay the fabrics out and unroll a yard or so to really see how they handle and perform. Crush a section of the fabric in your hands to see if the creases fall out easily. If they don't, the fabric will always look crumpled when worn.

TIPS

If you are new to sewing, start with lightweight cottons as these are durable fabrics and mostly inexpensive.

Avoid chiffons, satins, and other slippery fabrics until you are skilled enough to handle them, as they require more advanced sewing skills.

Keep leftover fabrics and scraps to make into patchwork pieces.

Fabric comes in standard widths. The most common widths for dressmaking and craft projects are 36 inches/ 90 cm, 45 inches/112 cm, and 60 inches/150 cm; soft furnishing and upholstery fabrics are usually about 50 inches/127 cm wide, but you may come across other widths, too. Commercial dressmaking patterns will tell you how much fabric to buy for a given width. For smaller craft or home furnishing projects where you're not working from a commercial pattern, you'll have to add up the amounts in the project instructions and work out how much you need yourself.

Remember to allow a bit extra if you need to match up the pattern across adjoining pieces. The same applies if you're buying fabric with a nap, like velvet, in which the pile lies in one direction and looks different when viewed from the other direction, or a printed fabric with a one-way pattern, as all the pattern pieces will need to be laid out in one direction. (With a solid color, you can turn pattern pieces upside down to achieve a more economical layout.)

On each bolt of fabric there should be a label that will tell you things like the fabric composition and whether it's washable; if you buy a fabric that's dry clean only, the cleaning costs can quickly mount up.

Be sure to buy enough fabric! It's better to have too much than too little. If you have to buy more fabric at a later date, it may come from a different dye batch and vary slightly in color.

Below: *A variety of fabric swatches.*
First row: Satin, blanket wool, cotton lawn, shirting cotton; Second row: Woven ticking, printed baby cord, felt, canvas; Third row: Printed furnishing linen, fine linen, linen union, cotton velvet.

SOME FABRIC SCIENCE

Fibers fall into four categories: natural, man-made, synthetic, and blends. The materials that make up fabric come from four main sources: animal (wool, silk), plant (cotton, flax, jute), mineral (asbestos, glass fiber), and synthetic (nylon, polyester, acrylic).

❖ **Natural fibers** are wool, silk, cotton, and linen.

❖ **Man-made fibers** (which can be made using natural materials like cellulose) include acrylic, rayon, and acetate.

❖ **Synthetics** are made completely from chemical sources and include nylon, polyester, and spandex.

❖ **Artificial fibers** are made from petroleum and only became available in the early 20th century.

❖ **Blends** are fabrics made up from any combination of the above sources.

Textiles or fabrics are made in various strengths, from the finest gossamer for underwear to the strongest canvas used for ship's sails. The relative thickness of fibers in cloth is measured in deniers; the term "microfiber" refers to fibers made of strands that are thinner than one denier.

NOTIONS

"Notions" are all the extra bits and pieces that you will need for your sewing project. The term covers everything from threads to interfacing, bias binding, closures like snap fasteners, buttons, and zippers, and decorative trims like lace, ribbons, or braid.

When you shop for fabric for a specific project, buy all the notions that you need at the same time.

CUTTING OUT

Many simple sewing projects only require you to cut out rectangles or squares of a certain size; for others, you will need patterns or templates. Here's a simple guide to how to work with them.

MAKING TEMPLATES

When templates are supplied actual size, all you need to do is trace them onto cardstock to make a template. Then draw around the template on the fabric and cut it out on a cutting mat, using either sharp scissors or a rotary cutter. Some of the templates used in this book need to be enlarged, and the percentage enlargement is given in each case. You may need to tape sections together to create the whole shape before you can cut the template out of cardstock or kraft paper.

PREPARING YOUR FABRIC

First, press your fabric to make sure it is free of creases. Straighten the fabric ends, either by snipping into the selvage, gripping each side of the snip, and tearing the fabric across, or (if the fabric won't tear easily) by marking a line at right angles to the selvages and cutting along it. This is so that the fabric can be folded evenly, with the grains aligned.

If the pattern tells you to cut "on the fold," fold the fabric in half so that the selvages meet along one edge.

Grain: This is the direction of the threads in a woven fabric. Pattern pieces are usually cut on the straight grain, which runs parallel to the selvage. On a commercial pattern you'll see a marking that looks like a line with an arrowhead at each end; when you pin the pattern to the fabric, make sure that this line is on the straight grain. The crosswise grain follows the weft threads and has more stretch than the straight grain. The bias grain is an imaginary line at 45 degrees to the straight and crosswise grains; it has the most stretch of all.

Selvage: These are the finished edges that run down the length of the fabric, parallel to the warp threads. The selvages prevent the fabric from raveling or fraying.

Warp and weft: Woven fabrics such as cotton are made from threads that run lengthwise (the warp threads) and threads that run crosswise (the weft threads).

Sometimes you may only have to make a partial fold; if so, make sure the distance from the fold to the selvage is consistent along the whole length.

POSITIONING THE PATTERN PIECES

Before you begin to cut out, place all the pattern pieces on the fabric, following any marked instructions about the grain line of the fabric. If the fabric has a printed pattern, make sure that the pattern pieces are the right way round. Commercial patterns have cutting layouts showing where to position each piece on the fabric, so that you keep wastage to a minimum. If you're not following a pattern, play around with different layouts until you get the one you feel works best.

CUTTING OUT

Pin the pattern pieces to the fabric, making sure you pin through both layers if the fabric is folded, or weight the pieces down. You can then either draw around the pattern with tailor's chalk and remove the pattern before cutting out, or simply cut around the pinned pattern with sharp fabric shears. Place one hand on the pattern piece and hold the shears in your other hand. Slide the lower blade under the fabric, making sure the shears rest on the table, and make smooth, long cuts using the full length of the blade.

HAND STITCHES

Most of your sewing will be done on the sewing machine, but it is essential to know the basics of hand stitching, too, as occasionally only a hand stitch will do. This section also introduces you to the wonderful world of hand embroidery.

Some hand stitches are functional—they're used for hemming or for closing up gaps, for example. Others are purely decorative. Hand sewing can be used at all stages of your project and it is essential to keep hand sewing needles in several sizes close by, always selecting the appropriate needle for the thread being used. Whether you're sewing or doing embroidery, some basic techniques apply.

THREADING A NEEDLE
For tangle-free sewing, cut the thread to no longer than 18 inches/45 cm. Any longer and it will form knots when working. Always use scissors to cut the thread—never break it.

The process of threading a needle is the same whether you are working with a tiny or a large needle. Hold the needle up against a white background so that the eye is clearly visible, then pass the cut end of the thread through the eye of the needle. If you find this difficult, use a needle threader. This is a piece of wire bent into a diamond shape and attached to a plastic or metal tab. To use it, pass the diamond-shaped wire through the eye of the needle, then loop the thread around the wire and pull the threader back through the eye; the thread will automatically come with it—and hey presto! Your needle is threaded.

If you're using perle cotton or stranded embroidery floss, you may find it difficult to get the relatively thick thread to pass through the needle eye. Here's a simple trick that's an alternative to a needle threader. Fold a single piece of sewing cotton into a loop and push the loop through the needle eye for about ½ inch/1 cm. Then loop the embroidery floss through the cotton-thread loop and pull the cotton thread back through the eye. The thicker embroidery floss will be pulled through at the same time.

TIP
If you're having trouble threading, pinch the thread between your thumb and index fingers until you can barely see the tip of the thread. Then, instead of trying to push the thread through the eye, push the eye of the needle onto the thread. Your fingers give the thread support, so it will not deflect or fray.

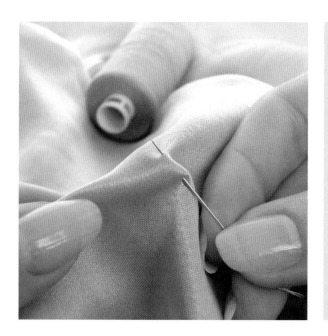

TIPS

Place a thimble on your index finger (or middle finger) and use it to push the needle through the fabric.

If you are using specialist threads, have them ready cut and prewound on a thread bobbin to save time.

When embroidering, use an embroidery hoop to hold the fabric in place. Hoops keep the fabric flat and taut, so that the stitches remain even.

Embroiderers and people experienced in hand stitching often draw the thread through a piece of wax, making it less likely to knot or twist.

STARTING AND FINISHING YOUR STITCHES

Before you start sewing, you need to tie a knot in the end of the thread to stop it from being pulled out of the fabric as you stitch. Loop the thread around your index finger, leaving a tail about ½ inch/10 mm long. Hold the cross of the loop between your finger and thumb and use the thumb to roll the thread up toward your fingertip, keeping the loop intact until it slips off and has formed a knot. Repeat to make a larger knot.

An alternative way to start sewing is to make three tiny stitches on top of each other at the beginning of the hand work. This method avoids a knot and makes for a secure start to any stitching line.

If you are right-handed, support the work in your left hand and stitch right to left using your right hand. If you are left-handed, support the work in your right hand and stitch left to right, using your left hand.

To finish off, work three small stitches on the back of the work and on top of each other, then cut the thread close to the last stitch.

If you make a mistake, unthread your needle and gently pull out the stitches, or carefully clip the stitches using your embroidery scissors and remove threads with tweezers.

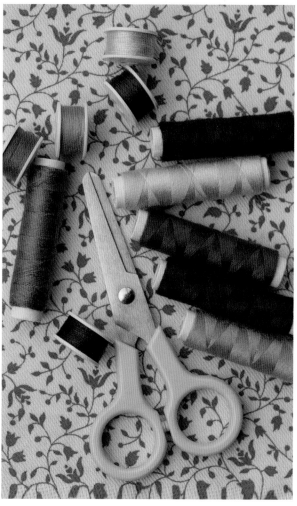

BASIC HAND STITCHES

Here are some of the most useful hand stitches. They're all very simple to do, and you will use them time and time again. For each of them, thread a needle with thread to match your fabric and make a secure knot at the end. (We've used a contrasting color of thread here, simply to make it easier to see.)

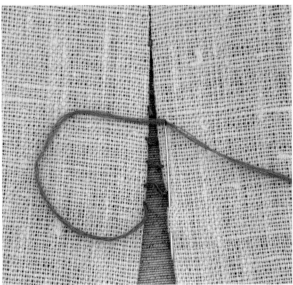

HEM STITCH OR CATCH STITCH

Use this stitch to hand hem or to catch any fabric to another. You can also use it on bias binding edging where topstitching isn't wanted.

With the wrong side of the work facing you, fold over and press the edge of the fabric to be hemmed and then again.

Insert the needle in between the layers of the first and second fold of the hem (or binding), and bring the needle out through the top fold so that the knot is hidden inside the hem.

Insert the needle just above the fold, catching a few threads from the main fabric.

Pull the thread gently and evenly through the fabric.

Insert the needle back into the hem channel and bring it back put about ¼ inch/5 mm farther along.

Catch a few threads from the main fabric.

Repeat until the hem is complete.

SLIPSTITCH

This stitch closes a space, creating an invisible join and is used when sewing up a gap left to stuff a project such as a doorstop or pincushion, or a gap left so that you can turn a project right side out.

When the seam is sewn and still on the wrong side, press it open, including the unstitched gap. (This creates a sharp crease that you can stitch along.) Turn the piece right side out.

At the beginning of the gap, insert the needle into the fabric from the wrong side, bringing it out on the crease line on one side of the gap.

Put the needle into the opposite seam, directly across from where it came out, and bring the point of the needle back out about ¼ inch/5 mm in front. Repeat on the opposite side, pulling the thread gently to close the gap.

Continue doing this until the gap is closed. Pull the thread gently to completely close the gap, and finish off either by making a knot or by weaving the thread back into the work.

> **TIP**
> Space your stitches evenly and do not pull the thread too tight or you will pucker the fabric.

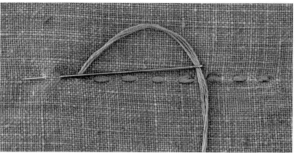

RUNNING STITCH

Hold the threaded needle firmly and push it in and out of the fabric until the needle is full, keeping both the stitches and the spaces between them on both sides of the fabric the same length.

Draw the needle and thread through, then repeat as necessary.

As a variation, alternate between short and long stitches.

Basting stitch, which is used to temporarily hold two pieces of fabric together before they are machine stitched, is a form of running stitch.

BLANKET STITCH

Blanket stitch can be used on a flat fabric as a decorative stitch, to edge a fabric, or to catch two fabrics together to form a seam. It works very well on felt, because the edges can be left raw and don't fray. This stitch was originally used to hem blankets—hence the name.

Bring the needle out at the edge of the fabric (or on the line where you want the base of the stitches to be). Insert the needle to the right of the previous stitch and above the edge (or at the top line, then bring it down at the edge of the work (or at the top line of stitches), keeping the working thread under the needle tip.

Draw the thread through to form a looped stitch. Repeat as necessary.

TIP

To practice your needle control, work rows of running stitch in different lengths. You may find it helps to practice on "aida" fabric, which is normally used for cross stitch; the fabric has gridded holes, making it easy to keep your stitch length consistent.

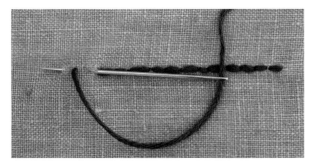

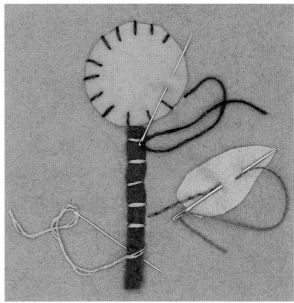

BACKSTITCH

Backstitch is a very strong stitch that is used, among other things, for hand stitching seams. It is also a useful stitch for embroidering things like flower stems. The stitches should be kept regular and short.

Work this stitch from right to left. Bring the needle out on the right side of the fabric about ¼ inch/5 mm to the left of where you want the stitching line to start. Insert the needle at the beginning of the stitching line, then bring it out about ¼ inch/5 mm in front of where it first emerged.

Draw the thread through. Repeat as necessary.

OVERSTITCH, ALSO KNOWN AS APPLIQUÉ STITCH

A commonly used embroidery stitch, overstitch—like backstitch—works well on felt appliqué.

Both are practical in that they hold fabric together well; they are also decorative, adding another dimension to the design—especially if worked in a contrast color and with embroidery silk/floss.

Bring the needle up on the right side of the work, next to the edge of your appliqué piece. Insert the needle down through both layers of fabric, then repeat, keeping both the stitch length and the spaces between stitches even.

FRENCH KNOT

French knots are ideal for embroidering the centers of small flowers.

Bring the needle up on the right side of the work, immediately to the right of where the knot is to be.

With needle pointing upward, twist thread twice around the needle. Push the needle back into the fabric as close to where it came out as possible. (You may find it helps to push the twists down the needle with your thumbnail as you do so.)

For a larger knot, wrap the thread three or even four times around the needle.

COUCHING

Bring the needle up on the right side of the work, next to the edge of your appliqué piece. Take the needle all the way over the appliqué piece and insert it next to the opposite edge; do not stitch through the piece being appliquéd.

This stitch only works for relatively narrow appliqué motifs, like flower stems. You can use the same technique to couch down thick yarns or threads.

USING A SEWING MACHINE

A sewing machine is a big investment, so before you buy one research the capabilities and make an informed choice based on your own needs. It is worth spending time looking at various types to find the right machine for you.

Sewing machines were invented during the Industrial Revolution and the basic principle of making a machine that would join two pieces of fabric together using a lockstitch is still the same today, even in the most technical of domestic machines.

The lockstitch uses two threads. One is threaded through from the top of the machine via the needle, and the second emerges from below the throat plate via the bobbin or shuttle, which is enclosed in its own case. Each thread stays on the same side of the fabric throughout the sewing, and interlaces and catches the other at the point where the needle pierces through the fabric. This forms a straight stitch, the length of which can be adjusted. The majority of machines also offer a variety of other stitches.

The essential things to consider are whether you want an electronic machine or a simple electric machine, and whether it has the following features:
- ❖ Reverse stitch
- ❖ Zigzag and other decorative stitches
- ❖ Zipper foot, buttonhole foot, and blind hem foot (some machine feet come as standard with the machine, while others can be bought separately)
- ❖ Thread cutter

TIP
Make sure the sewing machine sits firmly on your counter and does not wobble.

You should also consider how sturdy the machine is. A small, lightweight machine is great for most craft projects and dressmaking, but it may not be able to cope with sewing through several layers of relatively thick fabric, which you'll need to do if you're planning to make something like drapes.

TIP
Always work on a flat surface, with plenty of space around the machine for projects and for all the necessary sewing tools and materials.

THREADING YOUR MACHINE

Both the top thread (which comes from a spool on the top of the machine and is fed through the needle) and the bottom thread (which is wound onto a bobbin inserted into a space under the needle and needle plate) need to be fed through a series of tension disks and thread guides. The way you thread the machine varies depending on the model, so consult your machine manual for exact instructions.

Whatever model you are using, before top threading, always remember to lift the presser foot. This releases the tension disks so that you can pull the thread through easily. Also raise the needle to its highest point.

Bobbins are not normally interchangeable, so only use the ones recommended for your machine.

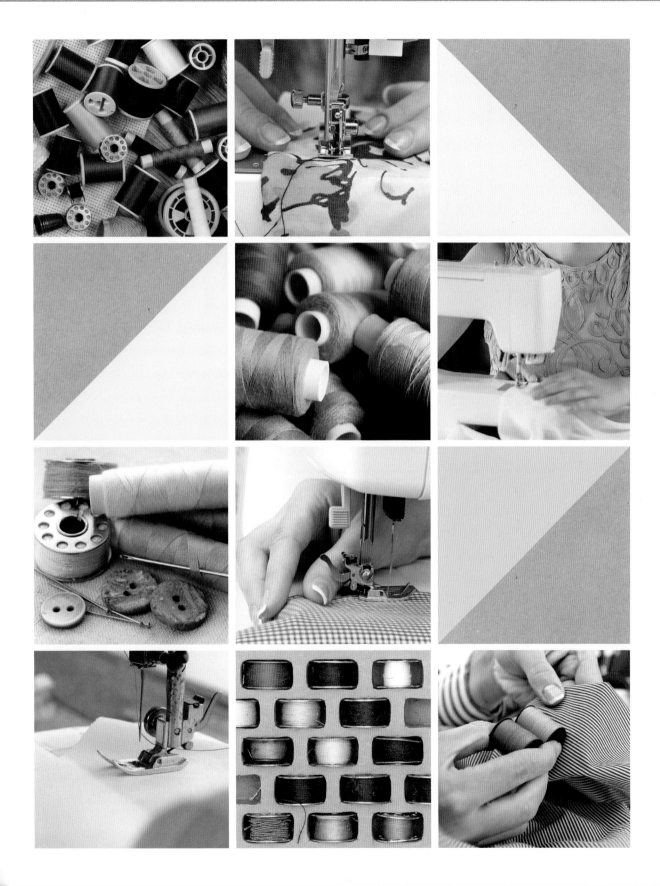

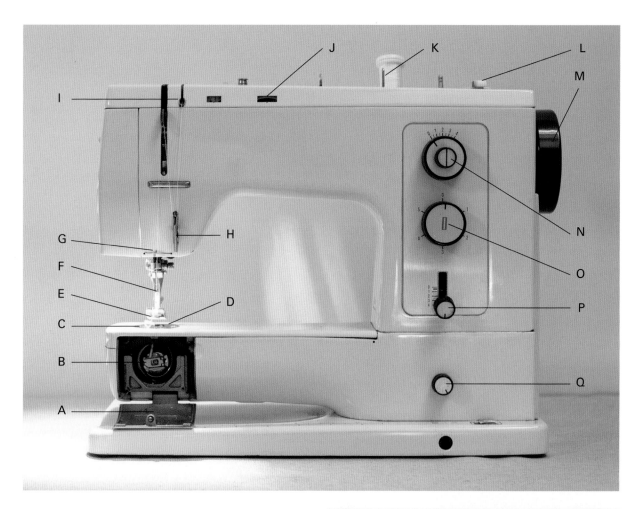

SEWING MACHINE ANATOMY

Sewing machines differ in design, but the basic features
will be similar to the model shown above.

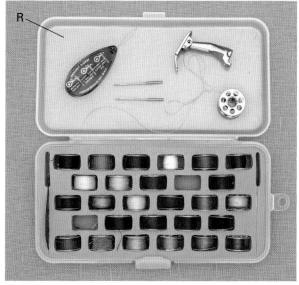

A   Shuttle cover (open)
B   Bobbin housing
C   Needle throat plate
D   Feed dogs
E   Presser foot
F   Needle
G   Thread guide
H   Thread tension
    regulator
I   Thread tension and
    thread guide

J   Stitch selector
K   Spool pins
L   Bobbin winder
M   Hand wheel
N   Needle displacement
    dial/stitch width
O   Buttonhole dial
P   Stitch length/reverse
    (when pushed up)
Q   Drop feed dial
R   Bobbin case *(right)*

TENSION

If your stitch tension is too tight, the fabric will pucker up as you stitch. If it is too loose, you'll end up with loopy stitches. When the tension is correct on both the top and bobbin threads, the connecting link between the two threads will sit centrally between the layers of fabric.

Before you start a sewing project, it is a good idea to work a sample swatch on a spare piece of the fabric that you are using for your project and adjust the tension if necessary.

ADJUSTING STITCH LENGTH AND STITCH WIDTH

A simple, inexpensive sewing machine can perform many sewing tasks and save a huge amount of time. The two most commonly used stitches are straight stitch and zigzag stitch, both of which are achieved by adjusting the length and in the case of zigzag, the width of the stitch.

These two simple tasks alone can make a variety of changes to the basic process.

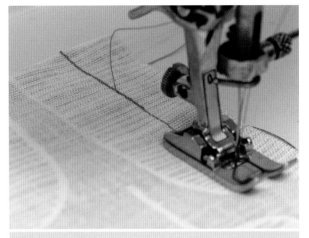

Straight stitch

SEWING A STRAIGHT SEAM

After you have threaded your machine, place the fabric under the needle about ½ inch/1 cm down the seam line, aligning the raw edge with one of the guidelines on the needle plate. If you follow this guideline, you will keep your seam an even width all the way along. (Your pattern or project instructions will tell you how big to make the seam allowance; it is usually ½ inch/ 1 cm or 5/8 inch/1.5 cm.) Lower the presser foot down onto the fabric.

All sewing lengths have a start and an end point. To prevent the stitch line from coming undone, reverse stitch almost to the top edge. (Your machine will have a lever or button that changes the stitch direction from forward to backward.) Stitch forward until you reach the end of your stitching line, then reverse stitch for about ½ inch/1 cm or so again.

TIP

If you are sewing with a very fine fabric, you may not like the way reverse stitching leaves a relatively large amount of thread that can show through the fabric. To prevent this, do not reverse stitch, but pull the top thread through to the back of the work at each end of the stitching line and knot it tightly with the bobbin thread.

USING ZIGZAG STITCH TO NEATEN SEAM ALLOWANCES

Zigzag stitch is a side-to-side stitch that is used to prevent a raw edge from fraying.

Adjust the width and length of the stitch to create the correct finish for the fabric you're using—refer to your machine manual for setting suggestions.

Zigzag stitch can be adjusted in length as well as in width. A wide stitch that is short in length looks like an embroidered satin stitch and can be used as a feature stitch as well as for buttonholes. A longer length and narrower width of zigzag stitch is used for neatening seam allowances.

If your pattern or project instructions tell you to press the seam open, zigzag stitch each side of the seam allowance separately; otherwise, stitch the two sides of the seam allowance together, as shown in the photo above right.

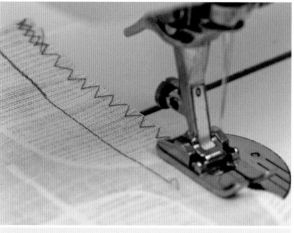

Zigzag stitch

NOTE: Zigzag stitch is also used to stitch seams where a straight stitch will not suffice (for example, for a stretchy fabric where a straight stitch will stretch the fabric).

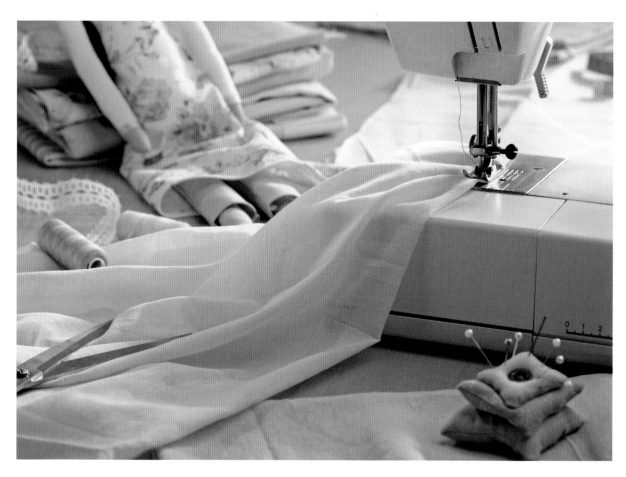

TURNING A CORNER

If you try to turn a right-angle corner while you are still sewing, the chances are you won't get a neat, crisp, 90-degree angle. Follow the steps below for success every time! You can use the same technique when stitching curved seams.

01. Stop stitching when you get to the cornering cross line on the bobbin cover. Leaving the needle down in the fabric, lift the presser foot and pivot the fabric around the needle by 90 degrees until the next seam line is aligned.

01

TIP

If there is no cornering cross line on the bobbin cover, stick a piece of masking tape in front of the needle, positioning it the width of the seam allowance in front of the needle hole.

02. Drop the presser foot.

03. Continue sewing until you reach the next corner, turning point, or end of seam, and either repeat or finish off by sewing backward for ½ inch/1 cm.

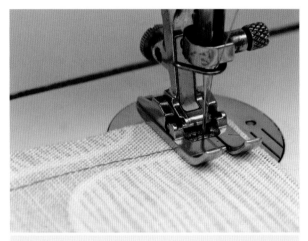

02

TIP

Never stop the sewing machine with the needle out of the work. Instead, always keep the needle in the fabric until the stitch line is finished.

MACHINE EMBROIDERY

A sewing machine can also be used to create decorative embroidery stitches. Freestyle sewing or machine embroidery is done by removing the presser foot altogether while still placing the presser foot lever in the down position.

For the best results, the fabric is stretched across an embroidery hoop.

03

PRESSING

Most sewing projects include a lot of pressing to produce a professional-looking finish. Don't skimp on this, as it's time well spent. Pressing your fabric as you go will ensure the best possible results for your project..

It's important to realize that there's a difference between pressing and ironing. Ironing is when the hot plate is passed back and forth to smooth out creases. Pressing means placing the iron on the fabric, holding it still for a few seconds to let the steam do its job, then lifting up the iron and placing it on another area.

If you do not have a steam iron, then a hotplate iron with a damp press cloth is a good alternative. Muslin, calico, or a clean dish towel all work well—just place the press cloth in cold water, wring it out before use, place it on the piece to be pressed, and then apply the iron. This creates steam, which helps to smooth away folds and creases from the fabric. Have a selection at hand in different fabric weights. A loosely woven piece will let you see what you are pressing and is well worth adding to your sewing kit.

TIPS
Position your iron and ironing board close to your sewing machine, so that you don't have to keep going backward and forward between the two. If space allows, you can even set your ironing board to sitting height right next to your work table and work from a swivel office-type chair, so that you can just swivel between the two without having to stand up.

Where possible, press in batches—stitch up several sections of the project, then press them all in one go to save to-ing and fro-ing. It may help to press your fabric before you begin cutting it out to ensure that you cut accurately shaped pieces.

TIP
Unless you want to flatten the fullness, do not press gathers or shirred fabrics—although a gush of steam from about 4 inches/10 cm away from the fabric works well.

HOW TO PRESS PROPERLY
Make sure the iron is at the right temperature for your fabric. Different fabrics tolerate different amounts of heat and steam—high for linen, low for silk and synthetics (that will mark or sometimes melt if the iron is too hot), and somewhere in between for everything else.

Don't be afraid of the steam, but handle with care and avoid placing your hands close to the iron plate when applying steam. Steam is extremely efficient in softening fabrics and will help mold it into the correct shape as well as being a great tool for shrinking a stretched piece of linen or saggy wool.

Seams can be pressed either open or to one side, so follow the instructions and press when told to do so. You might think you're saving time by not pressing, but it's a false economy to think that you can sew without first creasing a hem or turned edge.

Press as you go. If you stick to the basic principle of never crossing one seam with another until the first seam has been pressed, then you won't go wrong.

Keep the base of your iron clean so that you don't ruin your project when pressing. Buy an iron hotplate cleaner from your local hardware store to remove marks without damaging the surface of the hotplate.

Lastly… always turn an iron off when it is not in use.

GETTING
STARTED

Here's a selection of simple but stylish projects that you can make in just an hour or two—perfect for building up your sewing skills and giving you the confidence to move to bigger and bolder things! They make great gifts, too, so why not take a trip to your local fabric store, find some fabrics, thread up your machine, and give them a go?

Needle and
PINCUSHION CUBE

A pincushion and needle case are essential parts of your sewing kit and this design combines the two. Choose a robust fabric and make sure that the felt is good quality, as it will need to withstand lots of wear.

MATERIALS

24 x 4 inches/60 x 10 cm main fabric

4 x 4 inches/10 x 10 cm gray felt

8 x 4 inches/20 x 10 cm red felt

Matching sewing thread

Tape measure

Fabric marker or tailor's chalk

Fabric and embroidery scissors

Pinking shears

Iron and ironing board

Pins

Sewing machine

Crushed walnut shells or polyester toy filling

Hand sewing needle

Button approx ⁵/₈ inch/1.5 cm in diameter

FINISHED MEASUREMENTS

Cube measures approx 3½ inches/9 cm square.

TIP

Insert needles carefully into the felt, as they could easily get lost inside the pincushion.

PROJECT NOTES

❖ Thick cotton, linen, or corduroy are ideal.

❖ Take ½-inch/1-cm seam allowances throughout.

❖ Walnut shells are available at pet stores and are traditionally used as a filling to keep the pins sharp.

METHOD

01. Using regular fabric scissors, cut out six 4-inch/10-cm squares and a 2½ x 1-inch/6 x 2.5-cm strip for the button loop in fabric, one 4-inch/10-cm square of red felt, and one 3¼ x 3½-inch/8 x 9-cm piece of gray felt for the inside of the needle case cover. With pinking shears, cut an 3¼ x 3½-inch/8 x 9-cm piece of red felt, then cut along one short edge with normal scissors.

01

02

04

05

02. To make the flap/needle case cover, take one of the six main fabric squares. Working on an ironing board, fold over ½ inch/1 cm to the wrong side on all four sides and press, being careful to keep the corners sharp. Pin the gray felt to the wrong side of the fabric square, covering the folds.

03. Along both long edges of the button loop strip, fold over ¼ inch/5 mm to the wrong side and press. Then fold the strip in half lengthwise and press, so that it measures 2½ x ¼ inch/6 x 0.75 cm. Topstitch down the center, then fold the strip in half lengthwise again. Insert the ends of the folded button loop between the felt and fabric halfway along one 3 ¼-inch/8-cm side, with the loop protruding by about 1 inch/2.5 cm, and pin to secure. Topstitch all around.

04. Open out the fold on the right-hand edge of the fabric square. Match the straight edge of the red felt cut with pinking shears on three sides to the opened-out edge of the flap and sew along this side, along the crease line.

05. Take another red felt square and another fabric square. Sandwich the flap between these two pieces, with the right sides of the fabric pieces together; there will be a ½-inch/1-cm overlap at each end. Beginning and ending ½ inch/1 cm in, stitch for 3¼ inches/8 cm.

06. Attach three more fabric squares, one to each remaining side of the red felt square, in the same way.

07. Sew up the adjoining sides of the square in the same way to complete the cube, leaving a 2-inch/5-cm gap in the center of the last edge. Turn the cube right side out through the gap.

08. Fill the cube with crushed walnut shells or polyester toy filling. Neatly slipstitch the gap closed to achieve an invisible seam. Gently pat the cube into shape.

09. Holding the flap closed, mark where the center of the button loop falls on the adjoining side. Stitch on a button at this point.

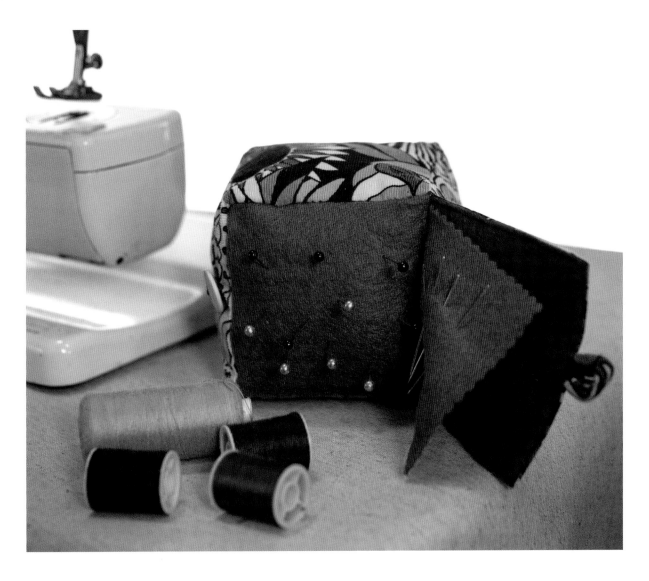

08

09

Contemporary PLACEMATS

Placemats can bring a clear style focus to a dining table and can be used for everyday eating as well as to dress up the table for a special occasion.

Simple placemat

An ideal starter project, this modern style of placemat (pictured left) is very simply hemmed on all sides.

MATERIALS

For one placemat:

18¾ x13½/47 x 34 cm inches fabric

Matching sewing thread

Ruler or tape measure

Iron and ironing board

Sewing machine

Fabric and embroidery scissors

FINISHED MEASUREMENTS

Placemat measures 17 x 12 inches/43 x 30 cm

PROJECT NOTES

❖ *Nothing could be simpler than this—just hem on all four sides and there's your finished placemat!*

❖ *Each placemat is cut from the fabric to show a different area of the bold pattern. The result is that each individual piece is unique and offers a contemporary approach to pattern matching.*

METHOD

01. Fold over ¼ inch/5 mm to the wrong side around all four sides of the fabric and press, then fold over a further ⅝ inch/1.5 cm and press again.

02. With the wrong side facing up, sew around all four sides, taking the sewing line to the outside edge in all four corners.

03. Press and use.

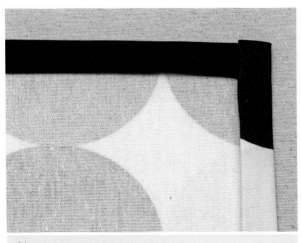

01

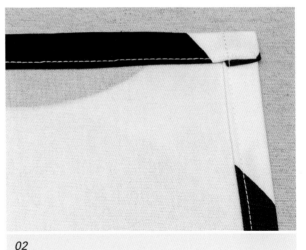

02

01

03

04

Fabric-backed placemat

This style of placemat is backed with a contrasting fabric and is very simple to make.

MATERIALS
For one placemat:
2 pieces of fabric, each 18¾ x13½/47 x 34 cm inches
Matching sewing thread
Pins
Ruler or tape measure
Sewing machine
Iron and ironing board
Fabric and embroidery scissors
Hand sewing needle

FINISHED MEASUREMENTS
Placemat measures approx 17 x 12 inches/43 x 30 cm.

PROJECT NOTES
❖ *This placemat has a contrasting fabric as the backing, which makes it slightly sturdier.*
❖ *For a more eclectic look, vary the fabric you use on the underside of the placemat: linen and ticking are both suitable.*

METHOD

01. Place the two pieces of fabric right sides together and pin all around.

02. Taking a ⅝-inch/1.5-cm seam allowance and beginning 8½ inches/22 cm in along one short side edge, sew all around, leaving a gap of about 3¼ inches/ 8 cm in one short side. Zigzag stitch around all sides, working either side of the turning gap separately.

03. Turn the placemat right side out and press the seams flat. Turn under the edges of the gap, then slipstitch the gap closed.

04. Press before use.

Embroidered
POUCH

Stitched entirely by hand, this project uses simple embroidery stitches and appliqué on wool felt to create a delightful pouch for your eyeglasses.

MATERIALS

8-inch/20-cm square of gray felt

3¼-inch/8-cm square each of jade-green, cream, and lime-green felt

Embroidery floss in yellow ocher, jade green, and orange

Fabric and embroidery scissors

Ruler or tape measure

Fabric marker or tailor's chalk

Pins

Embroidery needle

Button approx $^5/_{16}$ inch/8 mm in diameter

FINISHED MEASUREMENTS

Pouch measures 6½ x 4 inches/17 x 10 cm.

PROJECT NOTES

❖ Felt is an ideal material as it provides an even surface with no fraying edges.

❖ This design could easily be adapted to make a pouch for a cell phone.

METHOD

01. Cut a 6 x 4-inch/15 x 10-cm piece of gray felt for the front of the pouch and a 8 x 4-inch/20 x 10-cm piece for the back, neatly curving the top on the back piece to create the closing flap.

02. Cut the pieces for appliqué: a 1½-inch/4-cm circle of jade-green felt, a ½-inch/1-cm circle of cream felt, two leaf shapes 1½ inches/4 cm long from lime-green felt, and a 2 x ¼-inch/50 x 5-mm stem from lime-green felt.

03. Pin the large circle onto the front piece, 1¾ inches/ 4.5 cm down from the top short edge, then pin the small circle in the center of the large one. Using yellow ocher embroidery floss, work a series of straight lines in backstitch across both circles, varying the lengths to create the flower stamens. Using jade-green floss, couch the stem from the base of the circle to the right-hand edge of the front piece, curving it as you go. Work a series of French knots in orange all around the circle.

04. About 1¼ inches/3 cm from the bottom edge, appliqué the two leaves using overstitch and orange floss. Finally, work two stems in jade floss and backstitch, working from the base edge up to about three-quarters of the way along each leaf, curving each line.

05. Pin the two pieces of felt wrong sides together and blanket stitch all around the sides and base in yellow ocher floss. Blanket stitch across the top front edge and around the curved edge of the flap.

06. Make a vertical snip at the center of the curved edge for the buttonhole, then work a closely spaced blanket stitch all around the buttonhole in jade-green floss. Sew on the button. Press the pouch flat.

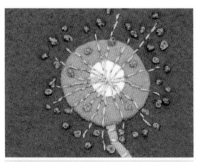
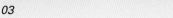

03

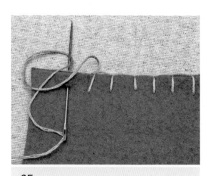

05

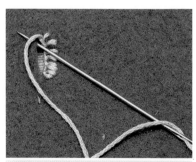

06

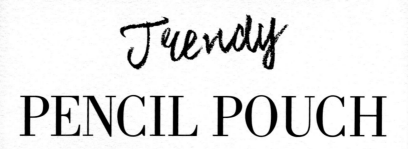

Trendy PENCIL POUCH

This simple-to-make pencil pouch uses a large-scale print, which gives it a very contemporary feel. This could be used as a change purse or a makeup bag.

MATERIALS

9 x 10½ inches/23 x 26 cm fabric

Matching sewing thread

Ruler or tape measure

Fabric marker or tailor's chalk

Iron and ironing board

Pins

9-inch/23-cm chunky plastic zipper

Zipper foot

Sewing machine

Fabric and embroidery scissors

FINISHED MEASUREMENTS

Pencil pouch measures 5 x 8¼ inches/13 x 21 cm.

PROJECT NOTES

❖ *Take ½-inch/1-cm seam allowances throughout.*

❖ *A furnishing-weight fabric is the best choice for this, as it will tolerate lots of wear.*

❖ *A chunky plastic zipper will give this versatile pouch a modern feel.*

TIP

If the zipper is the wrong size, cut a larger one down to size and sear the plastic teeth by gently melting them in a candle flame.

METHOD

01. On both 9-inch/23-cm edges of the fabric, fold over ½ inch/1 cm to the wrong side and press.

02. Place the fabric right side up on your counter, then pin the zipper right side down on top, ¼ inch/5 mm from the edge. Fit a zipper foot to your machine, then sew the zipper in place. Undo the zipper, then sew the other side of the zipper tape to the other 9-inch/23-cm edge of the fabric in the same way.

03. Keeping the zipper undone, turn the work inside out and press so that the zipper runs down the center.

04. Remove the zipper foot and fit a standard sewing foot. Pin and then sew the side seams, being careful when close to the plastic. Lift the presser foot and move it over the plastic teeth then continue. Zigzag stitch the seam allowances separately, then press the seams open. Press the long top and bottom edges of the pouch.

05. To make the boxed corners, work each corner as follows: line up the folded edge (the pressed top edge of the pouch) on top of the side seams and press; this makes a triangle shape.

06. Stitch a short seam across each corner, then snip off the tip of each triangle. Repeat with the pressed bottom edge.

07. Turn the pencil pouch right side out.

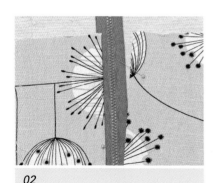
02

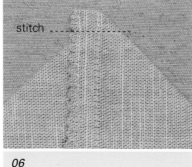
stitch
06

07

Embroidered WALL ART

Embroidered wall art adds a modern and unique feature to any interior. These three artistic designs make the most of any small ends of attractive fabrics that are left over from other projects.

PROJECT NOTES

❖ *The first hoop is simply a beautiful cotton floral; the second and third—a contemporary tree pattern and an embroidered dish towel—have both been appliquéd with felt birds, using a similar color palette to make a cohesive grouping.*

Floral fabric hoop

MATERIALS

8-inch/20-cm square of floral fabric
6¼-inch/16-cm embroidery hoop
Embroidery or other small, sharp scissors

TIP
Group together any number of hoops in different sizes to make a larger wall display.

METHOD

01. Undo the screw to separate the embroidery hoop into two parts.

02. Stretch the fabric tightly over the inner hoop, then place the outer hoop over the top to secure it in place, making sure there are no wrinkles in the fabric. Tighten the screw to hold the outer hoop firmly in place.

03. Turn the hoop over. Using embroidery or other small, sharp scissors, trim the fabric carefully all around the hoop.

02

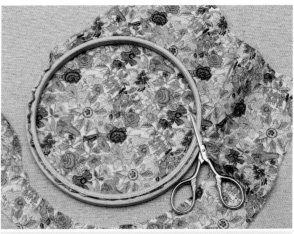

03

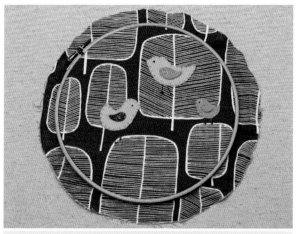

03

Appliqué birds hoop

MATERIALS

12-inch/30-cm square of patterned fabric

Felt scraps

3 colors of stranded cotton embroidery floss

Templates on page 126

Paper, fabric, and embroidery scissors

Fabric marker or tailor's chalk

10-inch/25-cm embroidery hoop

Pins

Hand sewing needle

04

05

METHOD

01. Using the templates on page 126, trace around and cut out three felt birds in different sizes and three wings in contrasting colors.

02. Undo the screw to separate the embroidery hoop into two parts. Stretch the fabric tightly over the inner hoop, then place the outer hoop over the top to secure it in place, making sure there are no wrinkles in the fabric. Tighten the screw carefully.

03. Pin the birds in place. Using two strands of embroidery floss, stitch all around each one with small overstitches using small, vertical straight stitches. Attach the wing with randomly spaced and angled running stitches to look like feathers.

04. Embroider the legs in backstitch and make three single stitches for the claws.

05. Turn the hoop over. Using embroidery or other small, sharp scissors, trim the fabric all around the hoop to create a neat finish when viewed from the front.

Preembroidered hoop

MATERIALS

10-inch/25-cm square of preembroidered dish towel

Felt scraps

2 colors of stranded cotton embroidery floss

Templates on page 126

Paper, fabric, and embroidery scissors

8-inch/20-cm embroidery hoop

Pins

Hand sewing needle

METHOD

01. Using the templates on page 126, trace around and cut out two felt birds in different sizes and two wings in contrasting colors.

02. Undo the screw to separate the embroidery hoop into two parts. Select an attractive section of preembroidered dish towel and cut roughly to size. Stretch tightly over the inner hoop, then place the outer hoop over the top to secure it in place, making sure there are no wrinkles in the fabric. Gently tighten the screw.

03. Pin the birds in place. Using two strands of embroidery floss, stitch all around each one with small overstitches, using small, vertical straight stitches, then attach the wings in the same way.

04. Embroider the legs in backstitch, making three single stitches for the claws.

05. Turn the hoop over. Using embroidery or other small, sharp scissors, trim the fabric all around the hoop to neaten the edge.

02

04

Simple
WRAPAROUND SKIRT

The wraparound skirt is a brilliant addition to any closet, and can be made in two different lengths. The contrast tape gives it a modern look, but you could easily make matching ties from the skirt fabric instead.

MATERIALS

Template on page 122 for the medium-length skirt, pictured, or on page 123 for the longer-length skirt

For the shorter version: 40 inches/1 meter fabric

For the longer version: 60 inches/1.5 meters fabric

80 inches/2 meters contrast tape, ¾ inch/2 cm wide

Matching sewing thread

Cardstock or pattern paper

Paper, fabric, and embroidery scissors

Tailor's chalk

Iron and ironing board

Sewing machine

Pins

PROJECT NOTES

❖ *Many cotton fabrics have a slight stretch in them, which works particularly well for this design, but a fine wool will work well, too.*

❖ *The medium-length skirt is pictured opposite.*

METHOD

01. Enlarge the template on page 122 or page 123 by 400 percent and make a template from cardstock or pattern paper. Adjust length to suit, if necessary.

02. Using tailor's chalk, draw around the template on the wrong side of the fabric and cut out.

03. Fold over ¼ inch/5 mm to the wrong side all around the outside edge and press, then fold over a further ⅝ inch/1.5 cm and press again. Sew all around the folded edge.

04. Cut the contrast tape in half. Pin one length to each top corner of the skirt, on the wrong side, overlapping it onto the side hem by about 1 inch/2.5 cm. Sew all around the overlapped section of each tape.

05. Cut the unattached end of each tape at a 45-degree angle to prevent it from fraying. Press and wear.

03

04

05

CONFIDENT STITCHES

Now that you've mastered the basics, why not tackle something a little more challenging? The projects here show you how to incorporate extra decorative details, like trims, appliqué, binding, and shirring, into your designs—and there's also an ever-so-easy patchwork technique that's just perfect for transforming precious vintage fabric scraps into a brand-new creation.

Linen-Backed
PILLOW

Pillow covers are the simplest way to add impact to any interior. Here, a bold geometric print is backed with plain linen in a bright, contrasting color.

MATERIALS

*15-inch/38-cm square of patterned fabric for
  pillow front*

15 x 24 inches/38 x 60 cm linen fabric for pillow back

Matching sewing thread

Ruler or tape measure

Fabric and embroidery scissors

Iron and ironing board

Sewing machine

Pins

14-inch/35-cm square pillow form

FINISHED MEASUREMENTS

Pillow cover measures 13 inches/33 cm square.

PROJECT NOTES

❖ *This design is easy to make with an envelope-style
back technique, so no zippers or buttons are involved.*

❖ *You only need one side of a pillow to be patterned—
so even if a fabric is expensive it's still worth
considering, as a plain back can be used.*

❖ *Linen is the perfect starting point for the back as its
simple weave gives a clean, contemporary feel.*

❖ *Take ½-inch/1-cm seam allowances throughout.*

METHOD

01. For the back of the pillow cover cut two pieces of
linen, each measuring 15 x 12 inches/38 x 30 cm.

02. On both back pieces, fold over ½ inch/1 cm to the
wrong side along one long edge, press, then fold over
a further ¾ inch/2 cm and press again. Sew the hem;
each piece now measures 15 x 10¾ inches/38 x 27 cm.

03. Place the patterned pillow front piece right side
up on your counter. Aligning the raw edges, pin one
back piece right side down on top. Repeat at the
opposite end; the hemmed edges of the back pieces
will overlap, forming the "envelope" into which you
can insert the pillow form.

04. Sew all around the outside edges, then zigzag
stitch around all four sides. Snip off each corner to
reduce the bulk.

05. Turn the cover right side out and press the seams
flat. Insert the pillow form and your bold, stylish pillow
is ready to use.

04

Pom-Pom
PILLOW

The scale of these colorful pom-poms makes for a designer-looking pillow cover that can stand proud in any living space.

MATERIALS

50 x 30 inches/125 x 75 cm fabric

44 inches/110 cm pom-pom braid (the braid with
   pom-poms can be bought ready made)

Matching sewing thread

Fabric and embroidery scissors

Ruler or tape measure

Iron and ironing board

Sewing machine

Pins

24 x 20-inch/61 x 51-cm pillow form

FINISHED MEASUREMENTS
Pillow cover measures 24 x 20 inches/61 x 51 cm.

PROJECT NOTES
❖ *Take ½-inch/1-cm seam allowances throughout.*
❖ *Embellished with a bright, bold trim, the simple weave of plain cream linen gives a contemporary feel.*

TIP
Always make a pillow cover the same size or ½ inch/1 cm smaller than the pad, not larger, because it will look loose.

METHOD

01. Cut out a piece of fabric measuring 25 x 21 inches/63 x 53 cm for the front of the pillow and two pieces measuring 25 x 15 inches/63 x 38 cm for the back. On both of the back pieces, fold over ½ inch/1 cm to the wrong side along one long side, press, then fold over a further 1 inch/2.5 cm and press. Stitch the hem; each piece now measures 25 x 13½ inches/63 x 34.5 cm.

02. Place the front piece right side up on your counter. Cut the pom-pom braid into two equal lengths. Pin one length to each short side of the pillow front, with the pom-poms facing inward.

03. Aligning the raw edges, pin one back piece right side down on top. Repeat this at the opposite end; the hemmed edges of the back pieces will overlap, forming the "envelope" into which you will insert the pillow form.

04. Sew all around the outside edges, then zigzag stitch around all four sides. Snip off each corner to reduce the bulk, taking care not to cut through the stitching or the pom-poms.

05. Turn the cover right side out and press the seams flat. Insert the pillow form to complete your colorful pom-pom pillow.

02

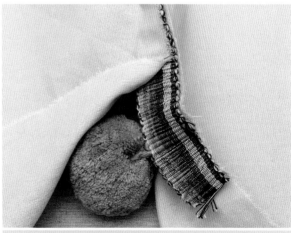

03

Appliqué Heart
PILLOW

Appliqués are cutout fabric shapes that are applied to a base fabric. Here the technique is used to decorate a simple linen pillow cover with funky heart shapes to create a unique and stylish design.

MATERIALS

52 x 20 inches/130 x 50 cm linen fabric

Matching sewing thread

Templates on page 126

Paper, fabric, and embroidery scissors

Cardstock or pattern paper

Fabric marker or tailor's chalk

Ruler or tape measure

Iron and ironing board

Sewing machine

Pins

18-inch/45-cm square pillow form

HOW TO WORK APPLIQUÉ

There are various methods of working appliqué. The most basic way, shown here, is to machine sew around a shape cut from an evenweave fabric such as linen, leaving a raw edge that will then fray when the fabric is washed and become a feature of the design.

Alternatively, stitch the motif in place by hand. Turn under the edge of the motif and sew all around it with tiny stitches, catching in just a few threads of both the base fabric and the appliqué.

Appliqué with felt is particularly satisfying, as the edges will not fray, allowing the motif to be attached with decorative embroidery stitches.

FINISHED MEASUREMENTS

Pillow cover measures 18 x 18 inches/45 x 45 cm.

PROJECT NOTES

❖ *Take ⁵/₈-inch/1.5-cm seam allowances throughout.*

❖ *Choose bold shapes for this type of appliqué: hearts are perennially popular, but stars or 1960s-style flowers with rounded petals would work equally well, too.*

METHOD

01. Cut a piece of linen for the pillow cover measuring 43 x 19 inches/109 x 48 cm. Using the templates on page 126, trace and cut out a selection of hearts in various diameters from cardstock. Trace around onto the fabric and cut out to create approximately 18 to 20 hearts with diameters of 1¼ to 3¼ inches/3 to 8 cm.

01

02. Fold over ½ inch/1 cm to the wrong side along both short sides of the linen and press, then fold over a further ¾ inch/2 cm and press again. Sew along both edges to secure the hem.

03. With the right side of the linen facing upward, mark the center of the work on both long side edges. Make another mark 9½ inches/24 cm to either side of the center mark. You will now have a central 19-inch/48-cm square. Arrange the hearts right side up within this section only. When you're happy with the arrangement, pin the hearts in place.

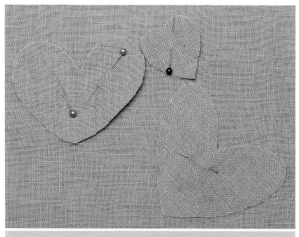
03

04. Sew around each heart, stitching between ¼ and ½ inch/5 and 10 mm from the edge.

05. When all hearts are attached, fold down the top edge along the line of the square that you marked out in step 03, then fold up the bottom edge (they will overlap) to make a 19-inch/48-cm square. Pin and sew both side seams, then zigzag stitch the two seam allowances.

06. Snip diagonally across each corner, taking care not to cut through the stitching. Turn the cover right side out and press the seams flat.

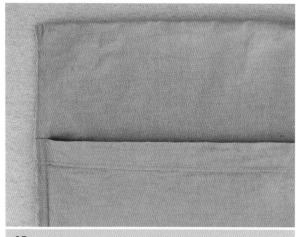
05

07. Wash the cover in a washing machine to fray the edges of each heart beyond the stitching lines. When the cover is dry, press it flat and insert a pillow form.

TIPS

If washing does not produce the kind of frayed effect you would like, gently tease out the loose threads beyond the stitching line with the tip of a needle; the machine stitching will hold the hearts securely in place.

If necessary, trim the frayed threads to the same length with a small pair of embroidery scissors.

07

Stylish DOORSTOP

Tired of doors swinging shut when you want them to stay ajar? A chunky doorstop in a bold, colorful print is the answer!

MATERIALS

12 x 40 inches/30 x 100 cm fabric

Matching sewing thread

Fabric and embroidery scissors

Tailor's chalk or air-erasable fabric marker

Long ruler

Iron and ironing board

Sewing machine

Pins

Zip-locked freezer bag

Uncooked rice, dried beans, or polystyrene beads
    for stuffing

Hand sewing needle

FINISHED MEASUREMENTS

*Doorstop measures 7 inches/18 cm high x 6 inches/
15 cm wide x 6 inches/15 cm deep.*

PROJECT NOTES

❖ *Simple to stitch, and with a sturdy handle so that
you can carry it from room to room, this project is both
pretty and practical.*

❖ *Take ½-inch/1-cm seam allowances throughout.*

❖ *Lightweight furnishing cotton is ideal for this project.*

METHOD

01. Lay the fabric on a flat surface. You will need to cut four pieces of fabric: one rectangle 24½ x 8 inches/ 62 x 20 cm for the sides; two squares, each 6½ inches/ 17 cm, for the top and base; and one rectangle 11 x 4 inches/28 x 10 cm for the handle. Using tailor's chalk or an air-erasable fabric marker and a long ruler, measure and mark out the four pieces on the wrong side of the fabric, then cut them out.

02. Along both long edges of the handle, fold the fabric over to the wrong side by ½ inch/1 cm and press. Fold the fabric in half, matching the long edges, and press again. Topstitch along both long edges.

03. Fold the top square in half, with right sides facing. Use a pin or tailor's chalk to mark the center of two opposite sides of the square. Matching the centers of the handle's short edges to the centers of the square's sides, pin and stitch the handle in place ¼ inch/5 mm from the edge.

TIP

Before you mark and cut out the fabric, select any motifs or areas of the print that you want to be prominent.

01

03

04. Fold and flatten the handle onto the top square and pin it to the square to avoid it catching in the sides when you sew the seams.

05. With right sides together, aligning the raw edges, match one side of the base square to one long edge of the rectangle for the sides. Pin in place, inserting the pins at right angles to the edge.

06. Place the machine needle ½ inch/1 cm in from the edge of the square and sew along the square for 6 inches/15 cm. Keeping the needle in the work, lift the presser foot, turn the work through 90°, drop the presser foot, and continue sewing along the second side for a further 6 inches/15 cm.

07. Carefully snip diagonally into each of the eight corners to allow the fabric to fold easily. Zigzag stitch around all the seams, stitching through both layers, to reinforce them.

08. Repeat steps 5–7 to attach the top square to the other long edge of the rectangle for the sides, leaving a gap of about 3 inches/8 cm in the center of one side. Turn the doorstop right side out through the gap, and press all the seams flat.

09. Place a zip-locked freezer bag inside the fabric case and pour the filling into this. You can use rice (uncooked), dried beans, or polystyrene beads as the filling. Slipstitch the gap closed.

06

08

Cool
SUMMER DRESS

Every girl needs at least one sundress in her closet for those balmy summer days and this one looks fantastic wherever you go, whether it's a chill-out beachfront café or a trendy city bar.

MATERIALS

Fabric (see Project Notes for details of how to calculate the amount)

Matching sewing thread

Ruler or tape measure and pencil

Fabric and embroidery scissors

Iron and ironing board

Tailor's chalk or bobble-headed pins

Shirring elastic

Sewing machine

Pins

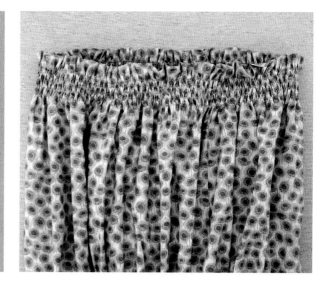

PROJECT NOTES

❖ *Choose your fabric carefully—ideally something that drapes well and will show the gathers to their best advantage. I used fine cotton lawn, but silk or viscose fabric would work brilliantly well, too.*

❖ *To work out the length of fabric you need, decide how long you want the dress to be by measuring from just above your bustline to the hem and add 4 inches/10 cm. To work out the width, measure around the fullest point of your bust and multiply by 1.5–2, depending on how full you want the dress to be (you might want to try shirring a small sample of fabric first to see how much it pulls in). Cut a piece of fabric to these measurements.*

❖ *If you haven't worked with shirring elastic before, practice sewing a few rows before you start on the garment. Wind the bobbin with shirring elastic, then thread up the machine as usual with cotton thread as the top thread. Sew straight parallel lines about 3/8 inch/ 8 mm apart, gently straightening the fabric as it comes out from under the presser foot.*

❖ *The oblong shape means it is easy to make the dress bigger or smaller, by increasing or reducing the width or length of the fabric. Straps can also be added, either as narrow bands or by shirring wider bands in true 1970s style.*

FINISHED SIZE

This garment is made to measure (see Project Notes).

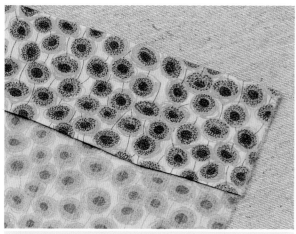

01

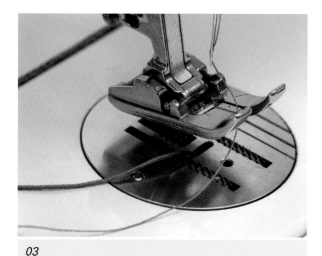

03

04

METHOD

01. Fold over ½ inch/1 cm to the wrong side along the top edge of the fabric and press. Fold over a further 1½ inches/4 cm and press again.

02. Using a piece of tailor's chalk or bobble-headed pins, mark each side edge of the fabric 10 inches/25 cm below the top fold; this indicates where to make the top line of shirring at the waist.

03. Wind the bobbin of your machine with shirring elastic, then thread up the machine as normal with cotton thread.

04. With the right side of the fabric facing upward, sew a line across the width of the fabric parallel to the top edge, 1½ inches/4 cm down, from one side to the other.

05. Sew three more rows above the first, spacing them ¼ inch/5 mm apart. Finally, sew a fifth row ¼ inch/5 mm below the first.

06. To sew the waist shirring, sew across the width of the fabric at the point marked with tailor's chalk or pins in step 02, then sew four more rows below the first, spacing the rows ¼ inch/5 mm apart.

07. Rethread the bobbin with cotton thread. Stitch a 2-inch/5-cm vertical line over each end of the shirring rows ¼ inch/5 mm in from the side edge; this secures the ends of your threads, preventing them from coming undone before you sew the side seam.

> **TIP**
> Line up the side of the machine foot against the previous row as a guide to help you space the rows of shirring evenly.

08. Fold the shirred fabric in half widthwise, with right sides together. Pin the side seam, matching the shirring lines carefully. Stitch, taking a ⅝-inch/1.5-cm seam allowance. Zigzag stitch each side of the seam allowance separately.

09. Fold over ½ inch/1 cm to the wrong side at the hem edge and press, then fold over a further 1¼ inches/ 3 cm, or the desired hem depth, and press again. Sew the hem edge from the wrong side, about 1 inch/2.5 cm from the folded hem edge.

10. Turn the dress right side out and press.

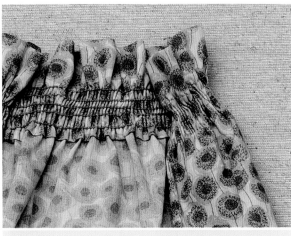

05

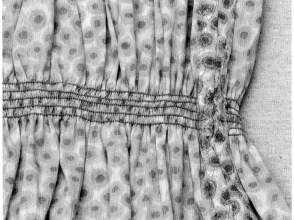

07

TIP

To make straps, put the dress on, measure over your shoulder from the top edge of the front to the top edge of the back (get a friend to help!), and add 2 inches/5 cm. Cut two strips of fabric to this length and 2½ inches/6 cm wide. Fold each strip in half, right sides together, and stitch along the long edge, taking a ½-inch/1-cm seam allowance. Turn right side out and press, with the seam running down the center. Pin the last 1 inch/2.5 cm of each strap in place on the inside of the dress and sew in place.

Vintage DRAPE

This simple patchwork panel of household linen and lace makes a beautiful and highly original drape for a bathroom or bedroom.

MATERIALS

Selection of linen and cotton pieces, including lace embroidery (tray cloths, doilies, and other pieces of household linen were used here)

Thread to match your fabrics

Iron and ironing board

Pencil and ruler

Pattern or brown paper

Paper, fabric, and embroidery scissors

Pins

Sewing machine

Pincer clips or small metal drape rings

Drape wire or thin rod

FINISHED MEASUREMENTS

This drape is a simple patchwork panel, so you do not need to add extra width to allow for a gathered heading. If the drape is to fit inside the window recess, simply measure the height and width of the window to work out your template size (see step 01); if it is to hang outside the window recess, work out the height by measuring from the drape rod or wire down to the bottom of the window ledge and add an extra 2 inches/ 5 cm or so to the width so that it does not look too mean and skimpy.

PROJECT NOTES

❖ *The interplay of different fabric textures adds visual interest, while the subtle shades of cream, ecru, and white create a sophisticated, contemporary feel.*
❖ *Ideal for a room like a bathroom, where you want privacy without blocking out the light.*

TIP

Before you start sewing, make sure that the fabric pieces are still flat. Repress them if necessary.

METHOD

01. Wash and press your fabrics. Work out how wide and tall you want the drape to be, then draw this measurement out on brown paper or pattern paper, and cut out the shape to use as a template.

01

TIP
Vintage lace-edged handkerchiefs and cutwork doilies that you may have inherited from a much-loved family member are perfect for this project, as the lace and cutwork sections will allow plenty of light through while the woven cotton around them affords a degree of privacy.

02. Arrange your fabrics by laying them out on the paper pattern, shifting them around until you have made an attractive arrangement of textures and shapes. Keep hemmed or finished edges on the outside edges of the drape, to avoid having to hem or tidy up any raw edges. When you're happy with the arrangement cut the fabric pieces to size, allowing an extra ½ inch/1 cm all around each piece (this can be trimmed down later).

03. Starting at the bottom edge, pin the first two pieces of fabric together, overlapping them by a minimum of ½ inch/1 cm, with the right side of the top piece against the right side of the underlying piece. (The overlap width may vary depending on your fabric type, so use your own judgment here.)

04. Using a straight stitch on your sewing machine, sew along the pinned edge about ¼ inch/5 mm from the edge, making sure you are sewing through both layers. If the top piece is lacy, use a narrow zigzag stitch and then trim to the edge of the stitching. Press the top piece back along the stitching line, so that it's right side up.

05. Continue pinning and sewing, two pieces at a time, until the patchwork drape is complete. Press the seams flat as you work so that the finished drape hangs well.

06. When you have finished, trim any loose threads from the front, then turn the drape over so that the wrong side is facing upward. Use your embroidery scissors to trim the fabrics close to the stitching lines and remove any other loose thread ends to keep the back looking neat, too.

07. To hang the drape, attach pincer clips to a drape wire or thin rod, or sew small metal drape rings, evenly spaced, along the top edge of the drape and then thread them onto the wire or rod. If the window is narrow enough, sew a drape ring to each side of the drape and hang from a small nail or hook, one on each side of the window frame.

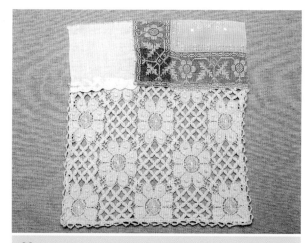

02

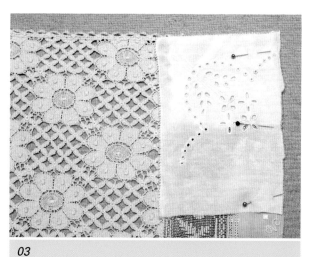

03

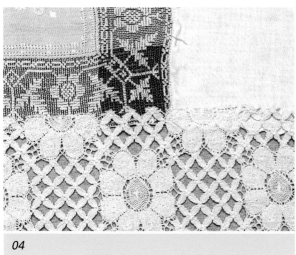

04

06

Coffee Press
COZY

Color choice is everything in this project! Here, a retro-style geometric fabric in zingy yellow and blue is offset by a vibrant orange edging and ties.

MATERIALS

24 x 6 inches/60 x 15 cm patterned fabric

12 x 6 inches/30 x 15 cm lightweight batting

52 inches/130 cm bias binding in a contrasting color

Matching sewing thread

Tape measure

Tailor's chalk or air-erasable fabric marker pen

Fabric and embroidery scissors

Pins

Sewing machine

Steam iron and ironing board

Hand sewing needle

FINISHED MEASUREMENTS

The instructions are for a 6–8-cup coffee press that is 6 inches/15 cm high, with a circumference of 11 ½ inches/29 cm. Adjust the width and height measurements if necessary.

PROJECT NOTE

❖ *Take ⅝-inch/1.5-cm seam allowances throughout.*

TIP

Batting is used as the middle layer in quilts to give them warmth and thickness—so it's the perfect insulating material for this cozy, as it will help to keep your coffee warm! It comes in different thicknesses, and is usually made from polyester, cotton, or a blend of fabrics.

METHOD

01. Measure the circumference of the coffee press, allowing a space for the handle, then measure the depth from base to top. Double the depth measurement. Add 1 ¼ inches/3 cm to both the depth and the circumference. Cut a piece of fabric to these dimensions.

02. Fold the fabric in half, so that it's the same depth as the coffee press. Cut a piece of batting to this size.

03. Pin the batting on one side of the fabric and sew along each vertical edge.

04. Turn right side out, then sew four vertical lines through the cover, spacing them evenly, catching all three layers together.

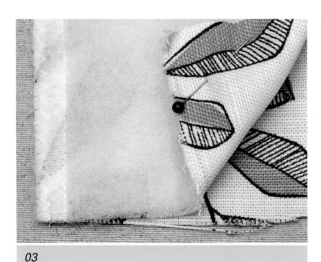

03

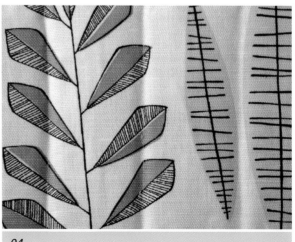

04

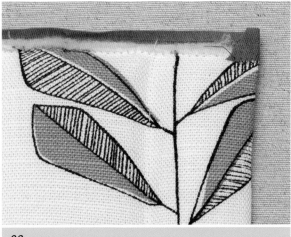

06

07

05. Open out the bias binding. With right sides together, pin it along the top edge, leaving ½ inch/1 cm overlapping at each end. Sew along the crease in the binding. Repeat at the bottom edge. Press the cozy.

06. Fold the binding over to the other side of the cozy, fold in the overlapping ends, and pin in place.

07. Slipstitch the lower edge of the binding in place.

08. Cut four 6-inch/15-cm lengths of bias binding for the ties. Fold each one in half lengthwise and stitch along the long edge. Mark four suitable places to attach the ties on the short edges of the cozy (two on each side) depending on the coffee press shape and handle placement. At each point, pin a tie to the wrong side of the cozy, overlapping it onto the fabric by about ⅝ inch/1.5 cm, and hand stitch in place.

08

Fabric
FLOWERS

Pinned to a jacket, or attached to a hat, bag, or hairband, these beautiful silk flowers create a finishing touch for any outfit.

Silky petal flower

Real flowers like roses or peonies often have slightly frilled petal edges. It's hard to create this by cutting the fabric alone, but carefully singeing the edges, as shown here, creates a wonderfully naturalistic effect.

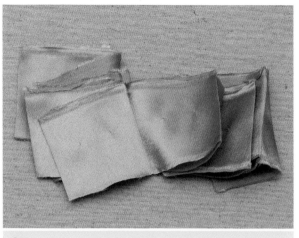

01

MATERIALS

15 x 1½ inches/36 x 4 cm synthetic silky fabric

Matching sewing thread

Fabric scissors

Hand sewing needle

Candle and matches

Brooch back, large safety pin or bobbie pin

Fabric glue (optional)

FINISHED MEASUREMENTS

Flower measures approx 3¼–4 inches/8–10 cm.

PROJECT NOTES

❖ *Use a synthetic silky fabric such as synthetic satin, tulle, or organza. When the edges are singed, the synthetic fabrics will melt to leave an authentic petal edge, whereas real silk will burn away.*

02

METHOD

01. Fold the strip over by 1¼ inches/3 cm, then continue folding it over in concertina folds right to the end until it measures 1¼ x 1½ inches/3 x 4 cm.

02. Using sharp scissors, cut a petal shape through all the layers, beginning ½ inch/1 cm up from the base edge. It doesn't have to be perfect—in fact, the odd mistake where a petal distorts can look quite effective and lifelike.

03. Open out and work a line of running stitch along the straight edge.

05

06

Silky rolled flower

This is a good way of using up fabric scraps, as it's made from just two strips of fabric cut on the bias. When the strips are coiled up, they fall into beautifully full flounces.

MATERIALS

Two bias-cut strips of synthetic silky fabric, each 20 x 3¼ inches/50 x 8 cm, one a solid color and one patterned
Matching sewing thread
Hand sewing needle
Fabric scissors
Brooch back, large safety pin, or bobbie pin
Fabric glue (optional)

FINISHED MEASUREMENTS
Flower measures approx 3¼–4 inches/8–10 cm.

PROJECT NOTES
❖ *Use a silky fabric for best results, as the fabric will curl and roll better than a thick woven fabric when cut on the bias—and it will shimmer, too!*
❖ *When choosing the solid color fabric for this project, pick out a color from the patterned fabric so that the two coordinate with one another.*

METHOD

01. From each of two different fabrics—one a solid color, one patterned—cut a bias strip measuring about 20 x 3¼ inches/50 x 8 cm.

02. With right sides together, taking a ⅜-inch/1-cm seam allowance, sew the two strips together along one short end, thus creating a 39 x 3-inch/98 x 8-cm strip.

04. Light a candle. Very carefully melt around the edges of each (material) petal by bringing the tip of the flame to the edges of the fabric until the fabric melts away from the flame; the synthetic fabric will become hard and slightly curled. The fabric should not burn or smoke—if it does, hold the fabric farther away from the flame.

05. When all the edges are singed, pull the thread to gather up the fabric, then begin rolling the length of the petals around on itself, loosening or tightening the running stitches to create an even tension. As you wrap, sew through the bottom edge to join all the layers together. Don't roll it too tight or too loose—the fabric will naturally form into a flower shape.

06. Once the flower is completely rolled, make sure it is secure by passing the sewing needle through all the layers from one side to the other a few times, then fold down some of the petals and manipulate the flower by hand to get the right look.

07. Attach the flower to a brooch back, safety pin, or a bobbie pin by gluing it in place or, if your brooch is the sew-on type, by stitching over the bar and through the fabric several times, taking care that your stitches do not show on the front of the flower.

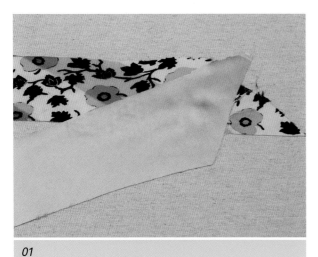

01

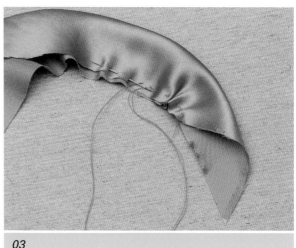

03

03. Fold the strip in half widthwise and work a line of running stitches by hand along the raw bottom edge, stitching through both layers. Do not remove the sewing needle. Slightly stretch the top layer more than the underside while sewing, as this will create nice diagonal gathers that will look good when the strip is rolled.

04. Pull the running-stitch thread to create gentle gathers, then begin rolling the bias strip into a coil. Pull the gathers as you wind, making some tighter than others, and stitch through the strip as you roll it around itself to create the flower shape.

05. Once the flower is completely rolled, make sure it is secure by passing the sewing needle through all the layers from one side to the other a few times, then fold down some of the petals and manipulate the flower by hand to get the right look.

06. Attach the flower to a brooch back, safety pin, or a bobbie pin by gluing it in place or, if your brooch is the sew-on type, by stitching over the bar and through the fabric several times, taking care that your stitches do not show on the front of the flower.

04

05

SEW
PERFECT

The real joy of sewing is that, because
there's an almost limitless choice
of fabrics and trims available, you
can create clothes, accessories, and
home furnishings that are truly
unique—no one else will have exactly
the same thing! These one-of-a-kind
designs will allow you to express
your personality and give full
rein to your individual
sense of style.

Makeup
BRUSH ROLL

This pretty accessory is a lovely addition to a dressing table and a perfect way to keep the bristles of the brushes in good shape.

MATERIALS

16-inch/40-cm square of fabric for outer roll

16-inch/40-cm square of contrast fabric for lining

Matching sewing thread

60 inches/150 cm bias binding, ¾ inch/2 cm wide,
in a contrast color

Pins

Fabric and embroidery scissors

Sewing machine

Steam iron and ironing board

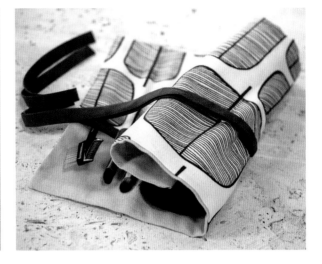

FINISHED MEASUREMENTS

Make up brush roll measures 14 x 9 inches/36 x 23 cm.

PROJECT NOTES

❖ *Take ⁵/₈-inch/1.5-cm seam allowances throughout.*

❖ *This handy makeup brush roll is also very useful when traveling and could be used to store eye pencils and mascara, too.*

TIP

Binding not only gives a professional-looking finish—it also strengthens the edges of the sections into which you're going to insert your brushes.

METHOD

01. With right sides together, pin the outer and lining fabrics together around the top and side edges only. Sew around these three sides, then zigzag stitch the seam allowances together. Cut the top corners off diagonally, taking care not to cut through the stitching. Turn right side out and press flat.

02. Cut a length of bias binding about ¾ inch/2 cm longer than the length of the pouch. Pin the bias binding across the open bottom edge, folding the ends in for a neat finish and sandwiching the two layers of fabric in between. Topstitch across the top edge, close to the edge of the binding.

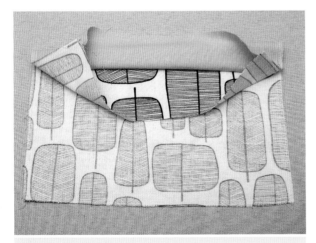

01

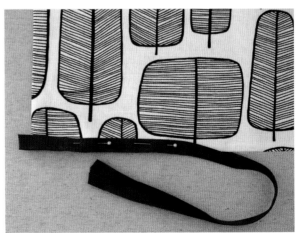

02

03. Place the square on a flat surface, with the lining side facing upward. Fold up the bottom 6 inches/ 15 cm, so that piece now measures 9¾ x 14½ inches/ 23.5 x 37 cm, and press the fold.

04. Pin, then topstitch, along the sides of the pouch to attach the front to the back.

05. To make the tape tie, tuck in the raw ends of the remaining bias binding, and then fold the strip in half lengthwise and pin along the unfolded edge, making sure all the pins face in the same direction. Topstitch along the length.

06. Mark the center of the length and pin this point of the tape to the back of the pouch 3½ inches/9 cm down from the top edge and centered on the width.

07. Turn the piece over and sew a vertical line from the center of the bottom edge to the top of the pouch, catching in the tape tie.

08. Sew a further set of lines to create six sections, varying the width to suit the size of your makeup brushes and taking care not to stitch in the loose ends of the tape in the process.

TIP
This is a very versatile design that can be used to store all kinds of things—you could easily adjust the size of the pouch and inside pockets to accommodate sewing materials, knitting needles, jewelry, or even pens and pencils.

07

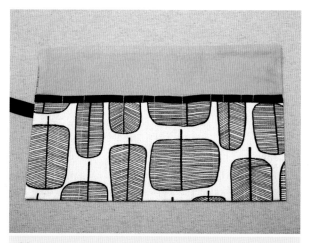

08

Simple
PATCHWORK QUILT

This project is extremely simple to stitch, so why not use all those left-over pieces of fabric that are too good to throw away and create a beautiful quilt that's not only practical but also truly individual?

MATERIALS

10 x 24 inches/25 x 60 cm each of 15 different fabrics, all of a similar weight

Sewing thread in neutral color

63 x 43 inches/160 x 110 cm cotton fabric for backing

63 x 43 inches/160 x 110 cm lightweight batting

Firm cardstock for template

Ruler and pencil

Paper, fabric, and embroidery scissors

Tailor's chalk or air-erasable fabric marker pen

Long quilter's pins

Sewing machine

Steam iron and ironing board

Hand sewing needle

FINISHED MEASUREMENTS

Quilt measures approx 60 x 40 inches/150 x 100 cm.

PROJECT NOTES

❖ *Take ½-inch/1-cm seam allowances throughout.*

❖ *Select the fabrics carefully. You will need 15 different styles to make a quilt like this one. Lay them out together and make sure that the colors and patterns don't jar or clash. Consider the scale of the print: if it's too large, it will be lost when cut into a square. Think about the color theme—a project with a consistent element will be pleasing to the eye.*

❖ *This is a great way of using up fabric left over from other projects. Alternatively, you could buy 15 "fat quarters" of fabric from a quilting store. Each one measures roughly 20 x 22 inches/50 x 55 cm (depending on the fabric width and whether it's sold in yards or meters), so you can get at least 12 squares from each one—leaving you with enough to make a set of matching pillow covers.*

❖ *Play around with different combinations, throw unusual fabrics into the mix, and incorporate favorite fabrics or material from a dress that reminds you of a special time in your life and you'll create a piece that is truly personal.*

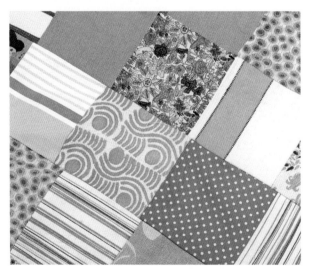

TIPS

You could use the same method, omitting the batting, to make a pillow cover. You will need four rows of four squares each to fit a 16-inch/40-cm pillow form.

For a slightly different, more random look, alternate squares and rectangles, keeping two edges the same length so that the patches line up.

METHOD

01. Using a ruler and pencil, draw a 4¾-inch/12-cm square on a piece of firm cardstock and cut it out to make a template.

02. Place the template on the wrong side of the first cotton fabric, as close to the side and bottom edges as possible, and draw around it with tailor's chalk or an air-erasable fabric marker pen. Repeat, butting the squares up against each other, until you have marked out ten squares in total. Cut out the squares.

03. Repeat step 02 with the remaining cotton fabrics, so that you have 150 squares in total.

04. Lay the squares out on a large, flat surface (use the floor if your counter is not big enough) in ten rows of 15 squares each and move them around until you're happy with the arrangement. Place the squares for each row together in a pile, making sure you keep them in the right order, then label each row.

05. With right sides together, pin the first two squares of Row 1 together along one edge, and sew. Continue in this way until you have sewn all the squares together in one long strip. Press the seams open.

06. Repeat step 05 until you have sewn all ten rows.

07. With right sides together, aligning the seams, pin Row 1 to Row 2 and sew. Continue until you have sewn all ten strips together, then press the seams open.

05

07

08. Place the batting on a large table or other flat
surface, and smooth it out so that there are no wrinkles.
Place the patchwork quilt right side up on top of it.

09. Place the backing fabric right side down on top and
smooth out all wrinkles.

10. Working from the center outward and using long
quilter's pins, pin through all three layers. Baste the
layers together in a vertical line from top to bottom
and then horizontally from side to side; finally, baste all
around the outside edge. Remove the pins.

11. Sew around all four sides, leaving a 12–16-inch/
30–40-cm gap in one short edge for turning. Zigzag
stitch around the outside edge, then trim off any loose
ends of thread or fabric.

12. Carefully turn the quilt right side out through the
gap. Press carefully but firmly all around the outside
edge. Remove all the basting stitches. Slipstitch the
gap closed.

08

11

Drawstring
LAUNDRY BAG

Have you got a stash of gorgeous fabric scraps that are too big to throw away and too small to make into anything useful? Combine them to make an eye-catching patchwork bag that will brighten up your laundry day no end!

MATERIALS

Fabric scraps in coordinating natural colors and patterns

Sewing threads to match the patchwork and lining fabrics

19 x 46½ inches/48 x 118 cm cotton fabric for lining

Two 32-inch/80-cm lengths of pink grosgrain ribbon, 1 inch/2.5 cm wide

Pencil and ruler

Brown or pattern paper

Paper, fabric, and embroidery scissors

Cell phone/camera (optional)

Sewing machine

Iron and ironing board

Pins

Safety pin

FINISHED MEASUREMENTS
Drawstring bag measures approx 18 x 22½ inches/ 46 x 57 cm.

PROJECT NOTES
❖ *Take ½-inch/1-cm seam allowances throughout, unless otherwise stated.*

METHOD

01. To make the patchwork outer bag, collect together fabrics that coordinate with each other. Using a pencil and ruler, mark out two 19 x 24-inch/48 x 60-cm rectangles on pattern or brown paper, and cut them out.

02. Lay your fabric pieces on the two paper patterns and decide where you want them to be. It is best to have at least two large pieces that cover the width at one end of each paper pattern; this will be the open top edge of the bag. It's a good idea to take a reference photo on your cell phone or camera at this point, so that you can remember where all the individual pieces go.

02

04

03. Now stitch the fabrics together to create two finished pieces of patchwork for the front and back of the bag. The best way to do this is to sew all vertical edges together, and then join your pieces horizontally.

04. Press all the seams open, then neaten all the seam allowances with a narrow zigzag stitch and press the pieces flat from the right side. Measure the two patchwork pieces and cut them both to 19 x 23½ inches/48 x 59 cm. Zigzag stitch around all four sides of both pieces.

05. Pin the two patchwork pieces right sides together, aligning the bottom edge. Sew along the bottom edge.

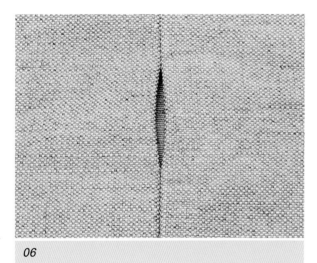

06

06. Beginning at the bottom edge, sew the side seam for 20½ inches/52 cm, reverse stitching at the start and finish to secure. Leave a 1½-inch/4-cm gap, then sew the rest of the side seam up to the top of the bag, again reverse stitching at the start and finish. Repeat on the opposite side of the bag. Press the seams open. Turn the bag right side out.

07. To make the lining, cut a piece of cotton fabric measuring 19 x 46½ inches/48 x 118 cm. Fold it in half widthwise, with right sides together. Sew down both 19-inch/48-cm edges to make the side seams. Finish with a zigzag and press the seams.

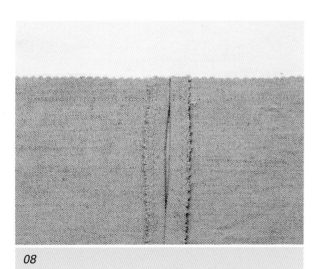

08

08. With right sides together, place the bag liner over the patchwork outer bag and carefully align the side and bottom seams. Pin the two layers together around the top edge. Beginning at one side seam, sew the two bags together around the top edge, leaving a 6-inch/15-cm gap for turning.

09. Turn the bag right side out through the gap, so that the lining is on the inside. Press the top seam, rolling it between your finger and thumb as you do so to prevent the lining from showing on the right side. Slipstitch the gap closed.

10. To make the channel for the ribbon, sew all around the bag, beginning at the top of the side-seam opening. Sew a second row of stitching all around the bag, beginning at the base of the opening.

11. Attach a safety pin to one end of the first length of ribbon. Starting at the left-hand side of the bag, thread the ribbon all the way through the channel until it emerges on the left-hand side again. Repeat with the second length of ribbon, this time starting and finishing on the right-hand side of the bag. Adjust the ribbon so that the same amount protrudes from each end of each channel, then tie the ends on each side together in a double knot.

TIP
If you use lots of different fabrics in a piece of patchwork, the effect can sometimes be rather busy and overwhelming. You can avoid this by choosing harmonious colors and offsetting the patchwork with a larger section of plain fabric, as we've done here.

11

Modern BEANBAG

Beanbags are so comfortable and are a great way of brightening up a living room or a child's bedroom. The outer case is easily removed—not only for washing, but also so that you can ring the changes by making a variety of patterned covers.

MATERIALS

3¼ yd/3 m calico, 60 inches/150 cm wide

3¼ yd/3 m patterned furnishing-weight or thick cotton fabric, 60 inches/150 cm wide

20-inch/50-cm square of solid-colored contrast fleece fabric for base

16 inches/40 cm webbing, 2½ inches/6 cm wide, for handle

Matching sewing thread

Templates on pages 120–121

Cardstock and pencil

Paper, fabric, and embroidery scissors

Tailor's chalk

Approx 24 inches/60 cm sew-on hook-and-loop tape

Approx 7 ft³/0.2 m³ polystyrene balls

FINISHED MEASUREMENTS

Beanbag measures approx 39 x 24 inches/100 x 60 cm.

PROJECT NOTES

❖ *Take ⅝-inch/1.5-cm seam allowances throughout.*

❖ *Because beanbags are likely to receive a lot of wear and tear, use a sturdy furnishing-weight fabric for the outer bag. Check before you buy to make sure that it is machine washable.*

METHOD

01. Enlarge the templates on pages 120–121 by 400 percent and make cardstock templates of the segment, top circle, and base semicircle shapes. Using tailor's chalk, draw around the templates on the wrong side of the appropriate fabrics and cut out. Cut six segment pieces in calico and six in patterned fabric, one top circle in calico and one in patterned fabric, and two base semicircles in the fleece fabric. You will also need one base circle in calico: fold the calico in half, place the straight edge of the semicircle template against the fold as marked, and cut out.

02. With right sides together, sew the six calico segments together. You may wish to double stitch the seams for added strength.

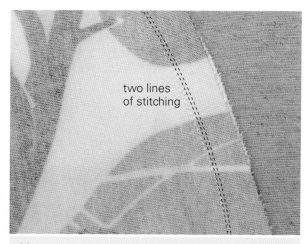

two lines of stitching

02

03. With right sides together, pin the calico top circle to the top edge of the calico segments and sew.

04. Repeat with the calico base circle, but leave a 12-inch/30-cm gap for filling.

05. Snip into the curved seams so that they lie flat, then turn the bag right side out. Carefully fill it with the polystyrene beads. When the bag is comfortably full, pin together the opening and slipstitch the gap closed.

06. Pin the webbing strap across the center of the patterned top circle on the right side of the fabric, 1¼ inches/3 cm from the edges. Sew twice across the short ends of the webbing to secure the strap in place.

07. Repeat steps 2–5 using the main fabric, being careful not to catch the strap in the stitching when you attach the top circle to the segments.

08. Along the straight edge of both fleece fabric base semicircles, fold over 1 inch/2.5 cm to the wrong side. Separate the two sides of the hook-and-loop tape. Pin in place, starting and finishing 1 inch/2.5 cm in from the edge and positioning one piece on the right side of one semicircle straight edge and one on the wrong side of the other semicircle; you may need to trim the tape slightly. Press the two halves of the tape together to make sure that the pieces align properly and reposition them if necessary. Separate the semicircles again, and sew all around the edge of each hook-and-loop strip. Join the two semicircles together again.

09. With right sides together, pin and sew the fleece base circle to the body of the bag.

10. Insert the stuffed calico bag inside the outer bag.

TIP
Filling the bag with beads can be a messy job, so do it outside if possible.

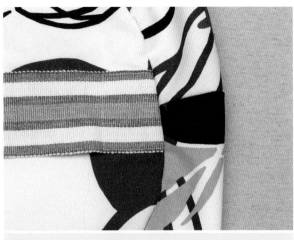

06

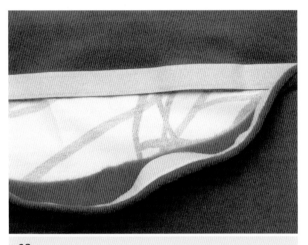

08

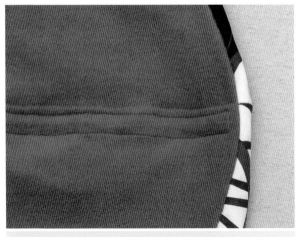

09

Slouchy
PAJAMA BOTTOMS

These simple pajama bottoms are great for slouching around in as well as for sleeping in. Each leg is cut in one piece, so there is no outside seam, which makes them a satisfyingly quick project.

MATERIALS

40 x 56 inches/100 x 140 cm fabric with directional pattern

18 x 22 inches/46 x 55 cm contrast fabric for cuff

10 inches/25 cm elastic, 1 inch/2.5 cm wide

Matching sewing thread

Template on page 124

Tracing paper, pencil, and paper for pattern

Paper, fabric, and embroidery scissors

Pins

Sewing machine

Steam iron and ironing board

Safety pin

FINISHED MEASUREMENTS

Pajama bottoms are one size only: size USA 6–10/ UK 8–12.

PROJECT NOTES

❖ *Take ¾-inch/2-cm seam allowances throughout.*

❖ *Crisp cotton will work just as well as a silky fabric, so once you've made one pair of pajama bottoms, why not try a few variations?*

❖ *The ties could be made in the contrast fabric.*

METHOD

01. Enlarge the pattern on page 124 by 400 percent and cut out.

02. With right sides together, fold the fabric in half lengthwise, so that it measures 40 x 28 inches/ 100 x 70 cm. Pin the paper pattern to the fabric following the straight grain and cut out.

03. With right sides together, pin the front seam together from crotch to waist. Repeat on the back seam. Sew the back seam.

04. Beginning at the crotch edge and finishing $2^5/8$ inches/6.5 cm before the waist, sew the front seam. Then sew the last 1½ inches/3.5 cm, leaving a gap. This makes the opening for the tie.

04

05. Zigzag stitch along all four seam allowances separately and trim the fabric back to the zigzag stitching if necessary. Press all the seams open.

06. With right sides together, pin and sew together both inside legs. Zigzag stitch the seam allowances on each leg together.

07. Cut two strips of contrast fabric for the cuffs, each measuring 8¼ x 21½ inches/21 x 54 cm. Fold each one in half widthwise, with right sides together, and sew the cuffs along each side seam. Zigzag stitch the seam allowances separately, then press the seams open. Matching the raw edges and seams, fold each cuff in half lengthwise, wrong sides together, so that the depth is now 4⅛ inches/10.5 cm. Press the fold.

08. Open out both cuffs. With right sides together, matching the inside leg seam with the cuff seam, pin one cuff around the bottom edge of each pajama leg. Sew using the sleeve arm of the sewing machine. Zigzag stitch around the seam allowance and press into the cuff i.e. downward.

TIP
Be sure to take your time matching the seams on the inside leg and the cuff in step 8—it will give you a much neater finish.

09. Around the raw edge of the cuff, fold over ½ inch/ 1 cm to the wrong side and press. Pin the turned edge so that it overlaps the seam by ⅛ inch/3 mm.

10. Press, then topstitch all around from the right side.

06

09

11. Fold and press over the waist edge to the wrong side by ¼ inch/5 mm, and then again by 1 ¼ inches/ 3 cm to form the channel for the ties. Pin and stitch the casing channel all around, beginning and ending ¾ inch/2 cm from the back seam, so that you leave a 1 ½-inch/4-cm opening for the ties. Turn the pajamas right side out.

12. To make the ties, cut two strips of fabric each measuring 30 x 1 ½ inches/75 x 4 cm. Fold over ¼ inch/ 5 mm to the wrong side along both long edges and press. Fold in one short end of each strip, then fold the whole strip in half lengthwise, pin and press so that the ties are ½ inch/1.5 cm wide. Topstitch along the long unfolded edge.

13. Sew the raw edge of each tie to either end of the 10-inch/25-cm length of elastic, using two lines of zigzag stitch. Working one side at a time, attach the safety pin to one end of the tie and thread into the channel through the back gap, coming out at the center front. Thread the other end of the tie through the channel in the opposite direction, again emerging at the center front. Machine stitch the gap in the back seam closed.

14. Making sure that the elastic is centered, sew over the back seam from the top edge of the waist to the bottom of the channel; this stops the elastic from slipping around.

10

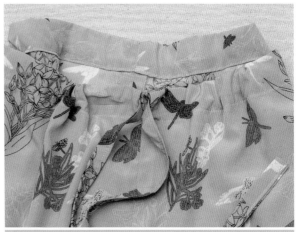

13

Linen
CROSSOVER APRON

This all-purpose, retro-style apron has a crisp, clean-cut style that reinvents the dowdy kitchen apron into a style essential. Made from soft linen, it has a casual, lived-in look but it would work equally well in a beautiful crisp cotton.

MATERIALS

48 x 55 inches/120 x 140 cm linen fabric

Matching sewing thread

Template on page 125

Tracing paper, pattern paper, and pencil for template

Fabric and embroidery scissors

Tailor's chalk (optional)

Iron and ironing board

Pins

Sewing machine

PROJECT NOTES

❖ *The easy one-size shape has a simple crossover back, meaning no fussing about with buttons or tape ties. The large front pocket can be divided as you wish, so that you can keep your phone or notebook separate from cooking items.*

❖ *Take ½-inch/1-cm seam allowances throughout.*

❖ *A plain fabric works well, but a striped, geometric, or floral fabric would look just as lovely.*

TIP

You could use a contrast fabric for the pocket if you prefer—perhaps a striped ticking, or even a sturdy printed cotton with culinary motifs such as cupcakes or kitchen gadgets.

FINISHED MEASUREMENTS

Apron measures approx 34 x 36 inches/86 x 91.5 cm.

METHOD

01. Enlarge the template on page 125 to 533 percent. Cut out the apron piece and facing. Cut out two straps, each measuring 30 x 4½ inches/75 x 12 cm. Cut out one pocket piece measuring 12½ x 10½ inches/ 31 x 26 cm.

02. To make the straps, fold over and press ½ inch/ 1 cm to the wrong side along both long edges of each strap. Fold the straps in half lengthwise, with wrong sides together, and press. Topstitch along both long edges.

02

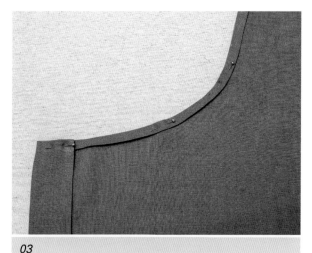

03

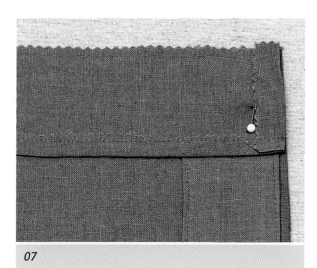

07

08

03. Place the main apron piece wrong side up on your counter. Beginning at the top edge, fold over ¼ inch/ 5 mm along the curved edges on either side of the apron and press. Fold over ½ inch/1 cm along both side edges of the apron and press. Fold over a further ½ inch/1 cm along the curved edge and press. Then fold over 2 inches/5 cm along the side edges and press.

04. Insert one end of one strap at the top of the side edge, slotting it between the layers of the 2-inch/5-cm fold. Pin or baste it in position. Topstitch along the curved edge of the apron approx ³/₈ inch/8 mm from the edge, making sure you catch the strap in the stitching. Topstitch down the side from the strap edge to the hem, 1¾ inches/4.5 cm in from the edge. Repeat on the other side of the apron.

05. Place the facing wrong side up on your counter. Fold the bottom edge over to the wrong side by ½ inch/1 cm and press, then fold over and press the two side edges by ½ inch/1 cm. Stitch along the bottom edge of the facing only.

06. Lay the apron right side up on your counter. Cross the right-hand strap over to the left-hand side of the apron, and pin the end to the straight top edge.

07. With right sides together, matching the top edges, pin the facing to the top of the apron, sandwiching the straps in between. Stitch along the top edge.

08. Open out and press the seam open.

09. Turn the facing to the wrong side, pinning along both side edges.

10. Work a second row of topstitching along both curved edges, stitching 1/8 inch/3 mm from the outside edge parallel with the first row.

11. Now attach the pocket. Fold over ½ inch/1 cm to the wrong side along the top edge of the pocket, and press. Work clockwise around the pocket, folding over and pressing a ½-inch/1-cm hem on each side. Finally fold over the top edge a second time by 1¼ inches/3 cm and press. Stitch along the top edge close to the fold to create a hem.

12. The pocket position is up to you—some people prefer to place it more toward the sides than the front, so put the apron on and work out the best pocket position. Pin and baste the pocket to the apron, making sure that the top edge of the pocket matches the straight grain of the fabric. Sew around the side and bottom edges of the pocket.

13. Finally, sew a vertical row of stitching from the bottom to the top of the pocket 4 inches/10 cm in to create two separate pocket areas. NB It is important to sew upward from the bottom edge of the pocket to the top to avoid the pocket puckering if the linen stretches.

14. Turn up the hem by folding over ½ inch/1 cm, then a further 2 inches/5 cm, press, and machine stitch.

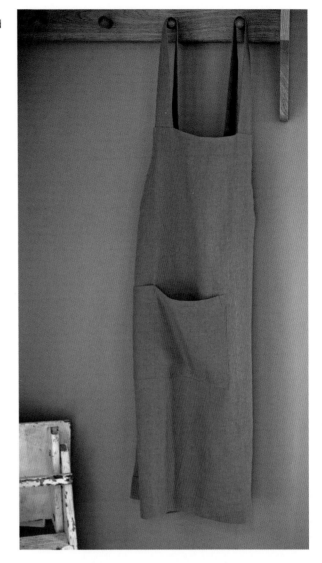

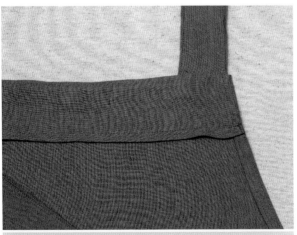

10

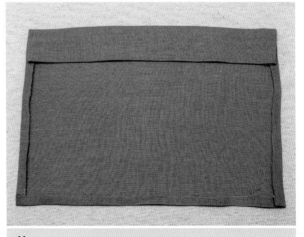

11

Lined
BEACH BAG

Made from a bold geometric print with a zingy tropical-orange lining, this ingenious beach bag is both chic and very practical.

MATERIALS

40 x 52 inches/100 x 130 cm sturdy cotton or light cotton canvas fabric for the outer bag

28 x 55-inch/70 x 140-cm towel for lining

40 inches/1 m of twisted cord, 5/8 inch/1.5 cm in diameter, for the handles

Matching sewing threads

Pencil or tailor's chalk

Ruler or tape measure

Fabric and embroidery scissors

Iron and ironing board

Sewing machine

Pins

Eyelet setting tool

4 x ¾-inch/2-cm eyelets

FINISHED MEASUREMENTS

Beach bag measures approx 25 x 17 inches/63 x 43 cm.

PROJECT NOTES

❖ *Take ½-inch/1-cm seam allowances throughout, unless otherwise stated.*

❖ *The lining is toweling, which is perfect for carrying your wet swimsuit back to the hotel.*

❖ *Using a ready-made towel means that you can use the hemmed edges of the towel for the top edge of the pocket and the bag. If you are not using a towel, cut the lining the same size as the outer bag and the lining pocket to 12½ x 8 inches/31 x 20 cm, and sew a ¾-inch/2-cm hem on one long edge.*

❖ *If you can't find thick enough cord for the handle, then twist thinner piping cord together.*

TIP

Add another pocket to the back of the bag, perhaps subdividing it into two or three sections so that you've got different compartments for suntan lotion, cell phone, or tablet, and a cool drink.

METHOD

01. From the outer fabric, cut one piece for the bag measuring 22 x 51 inches/56 x 130 cm and an outer pocket measuring 6¼ x 8 inches/16 x 20 cm. From the towel, cut one piece for the lining measuring 21½ x 52 inches/54 x 130 cm, using a hemmed edge of the towel as one of your long edges; this edge will be the top edge of the lining. From the rest of the towel, cut an inner pocket measuring 12½ x 7 inches/31 x 18 cm, again cutting one long side along an already hemmed edge.

02. Turn over ½ inch/1 cm to the wrong side all around the outer pocket and press, then turn over a further 1 inch/2.5 cm along the top edge and press again. Sew along the top edge close to the fold.

03. On the toweling inner pocket, turn over ½ inch/ 1 cm around the side and bottom edges and press.

04. Lay the outer fabric right side up on your counter and pin the outer pocket in place, 15½ inches/39 cm in from the right-hand side and 6¼ inches/16 cm down from top edge. Sew around the sides and bottom edge as close to the edge as possible, stitching an optional triangle at both top edges for extra strength.

04

05. With right sides together, pin the inside toweling pocket to the toweling lining, positioning it 6½ inches/ 17 cm in from the right-hand side, with the prehemmed top edge of the pocket 4 inches/10 cm below the hemmed top edge of the lining. Sew around the sides and bottom edge of the pocket, then sew a vertical line down the pocket 3½ inches/8.5 cm from the left-hand side, dividing the pocket into two.

06. Fold both the outer bag and the lining pieces in half widthwise, right sides together. On each one, sew along the side and bottom edges, taking a ¾-inch/2-cm seam allowance. Zigzag stitch along both edges. On the outer bag only, fold over ¾ inch/2 cm to the wrong side all around the top edge and press.

07. To make the base of the bag, at the bottom of the outer bag, position one side seam so that it sits directly over the bottom seam and press; the corner now forms a triangle. Pin the two layers of fabric together. Measure 2¾ inches/7 cm from the tip of the triangle and draw a straight line across the fabric at that point. Sew along your drawn line, snip off the excess fabric, and zigzag stitch across the raw edges to neaten. Repeat on the opposite corner.

08. Repeat step 07 on both corners of the toweling lining.

09. Turn both the outer bag and lining right side out and press all seams.

10. Place the lining inside the outer bag, wrong sides together, matching the side seams, bottom corners, and top edges. Pin both pieces together carefully around the top edge and topstitch 1/8 inch/3 mm from the top edge.

11. On both sides of the bag, measure 1¼ inches/3 cm down from the top edge and 8 inches/20 cm in from each side, and mark these points with a pencil or tailor's chalk. Following the manufacturer's instructions, insert an eyelet at each marked point.

12. Cut the twisted cord for the handles into two equal lengths. Working from the front of the bag, thread one length through one eyelet and bring it out through the other; tie both ends of the cord in a knot on the front of the bag to secure. Repeat on the back of the bag.

TIP

Depending on whether you want the bag to fit snugly under your arm or to hang lower down by your side, you may need to adjust the length of the straps.

05

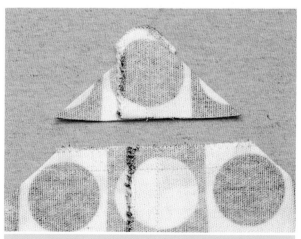

07

09

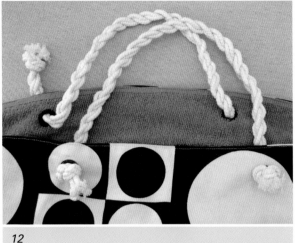

12

TEMPLATES

The following pages contain all the templates you need for the projects in this book. Some templates need to be enlarged. For details of how to do this and transfer them to sturdy cardstock so that they can be reused, turn to page 22.

MODERN BEANBAG

See project on page 104

Enlarge templates to 400 percent

The handy background grid will help you to align enlarged template pieces when joining them together.

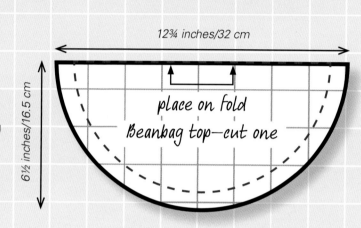

12¾ inches/32 cm

6½ inches/16.5 cm

place on fold

Beanbag top—cut one

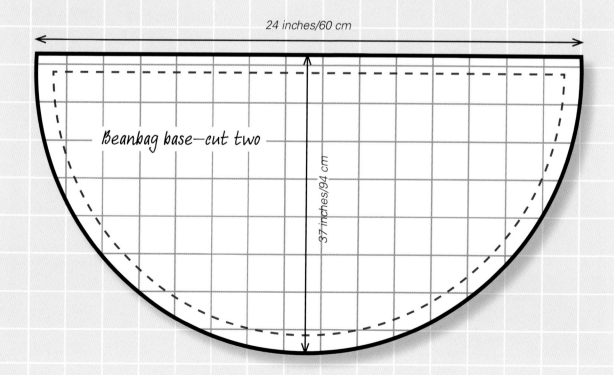

24 inches/60 cm

37 inches/94 cm

Beanbag base—cut two

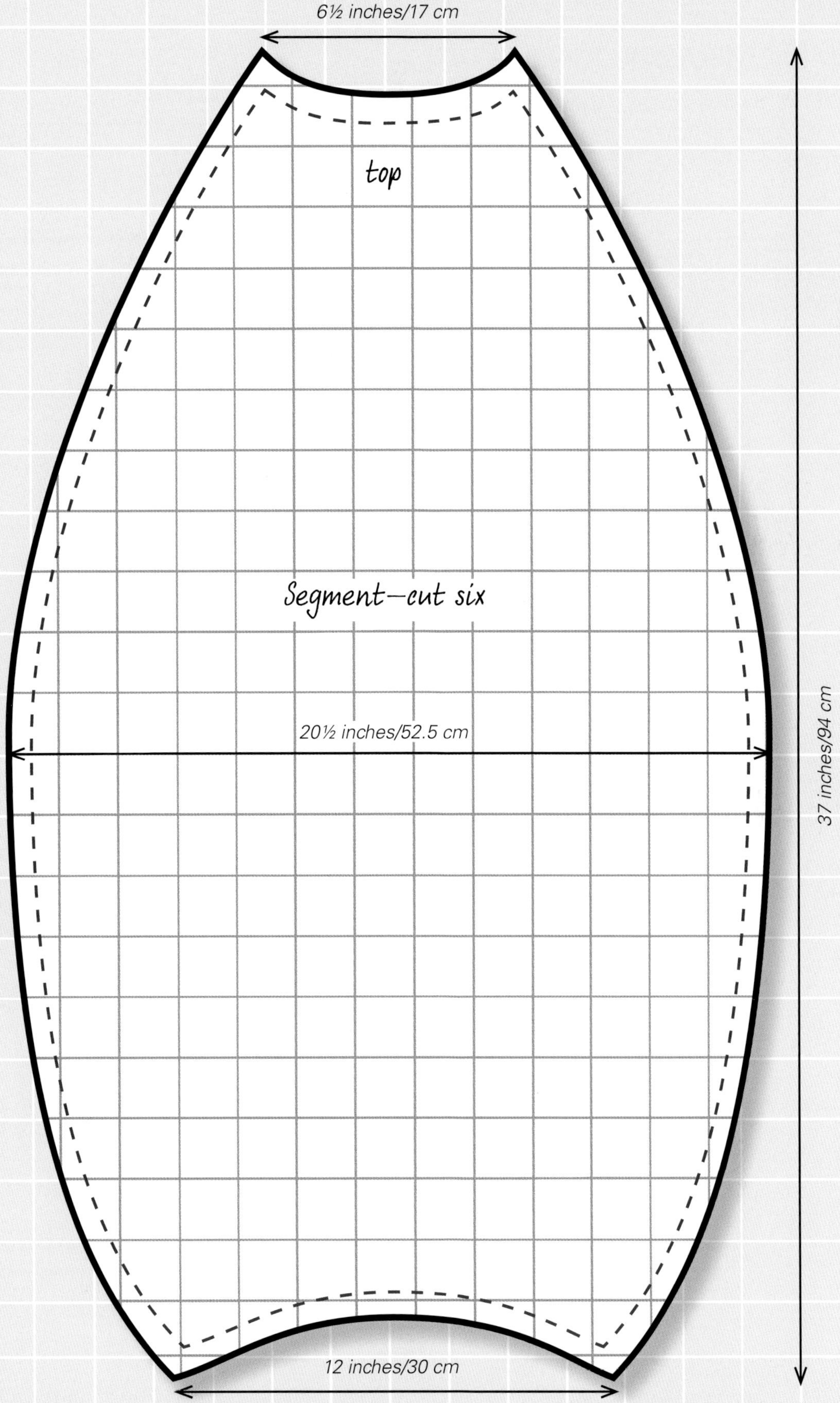

6½ inches/17 cm

top

Segment—cut six

20½ inches/52.5 cm

37 inches/94 cm

12 inches/30 cm

SIMPLE WRAPAROUND SKIRT

See project on page 56

Enlarge template to 400 percent

The handy background grid
will help you to align enlarged
template pieces when joining
them together.

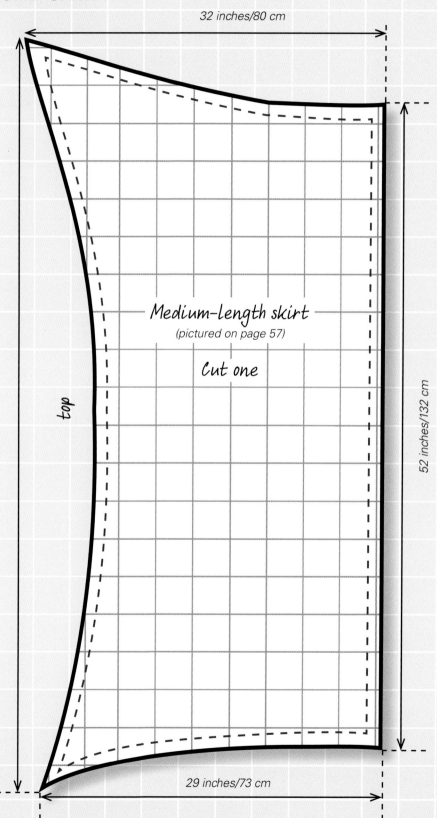

32 inches/80 cm

Medium-length skirt
(pictured on page 57)

Cut one

top

52 inches/132 cm

29 inches/73 cm

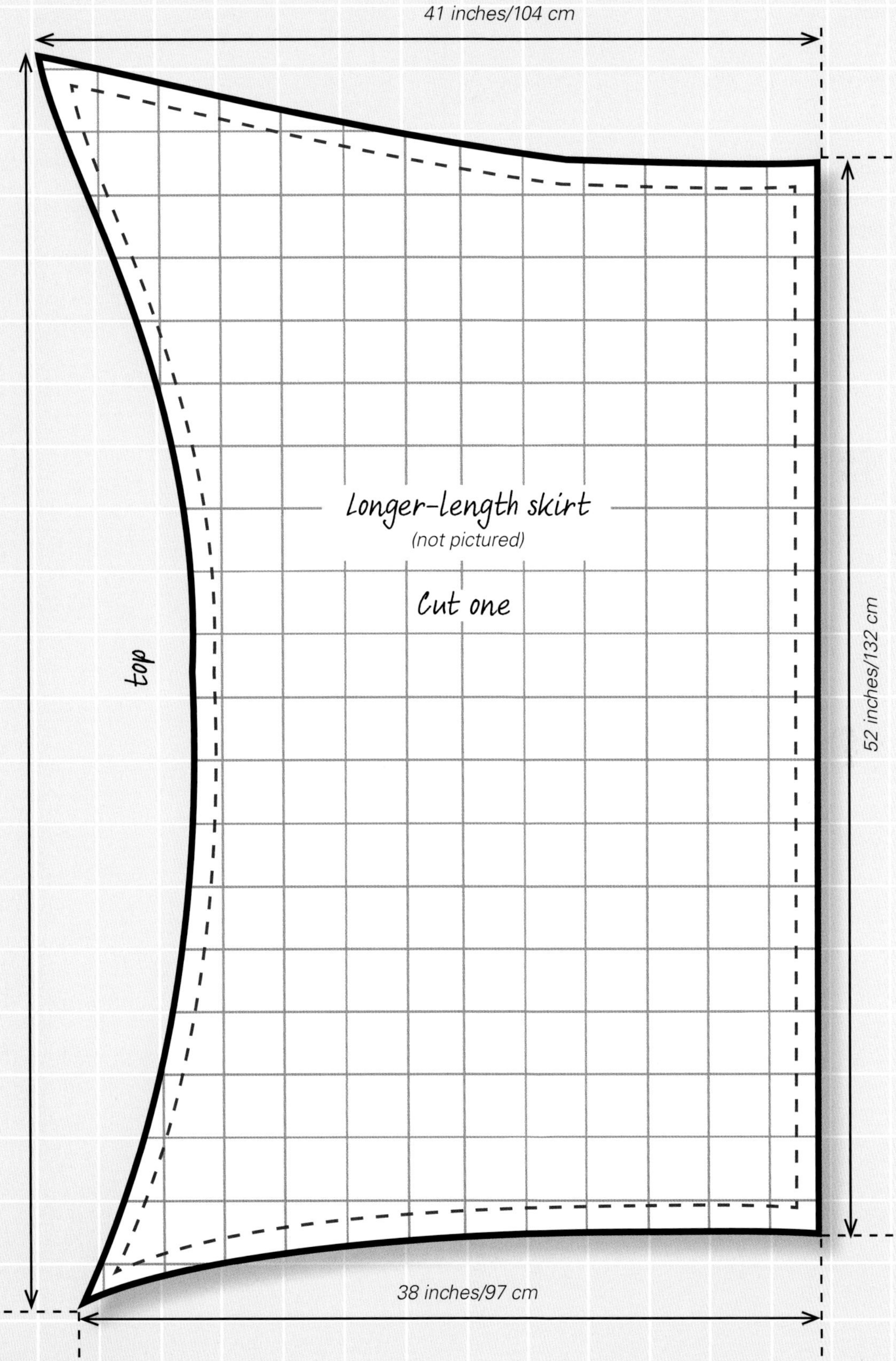

41 inches/104 cm

Longer-length skirt
(not pictured)

Cut one

top

52 inches/132 cm

38 inches/97 cm

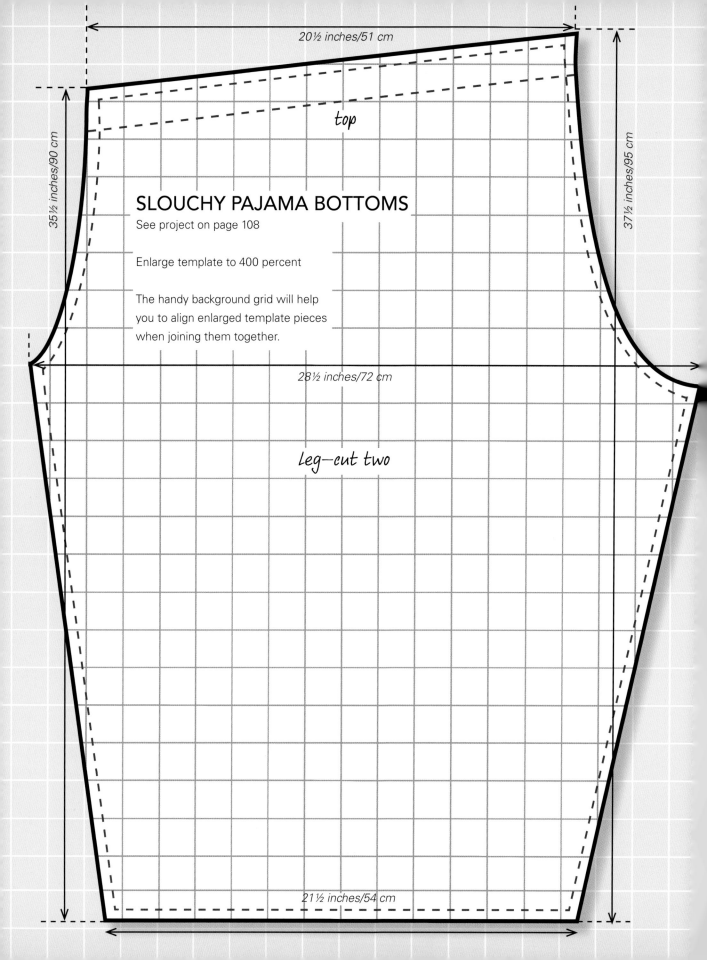

20½ inches/51 cm

top

35½ inches/90 cm

37½ inches/95 cm

SLOUCHY PAJAMA BOTTOMS
See project on page 108

Enlarge template to 400 percent

The handy background grid will help
you to align enlarged template pieces
when joining them together.

28½ inches/72 cm

leg—cut two

21½ inches/54 cm

LINEN CROSSOVER APRON

See project on page 112

Enlarge template to 533 percent

The handy background grid
will help you to align enlarged
template pieces when joining
them together.

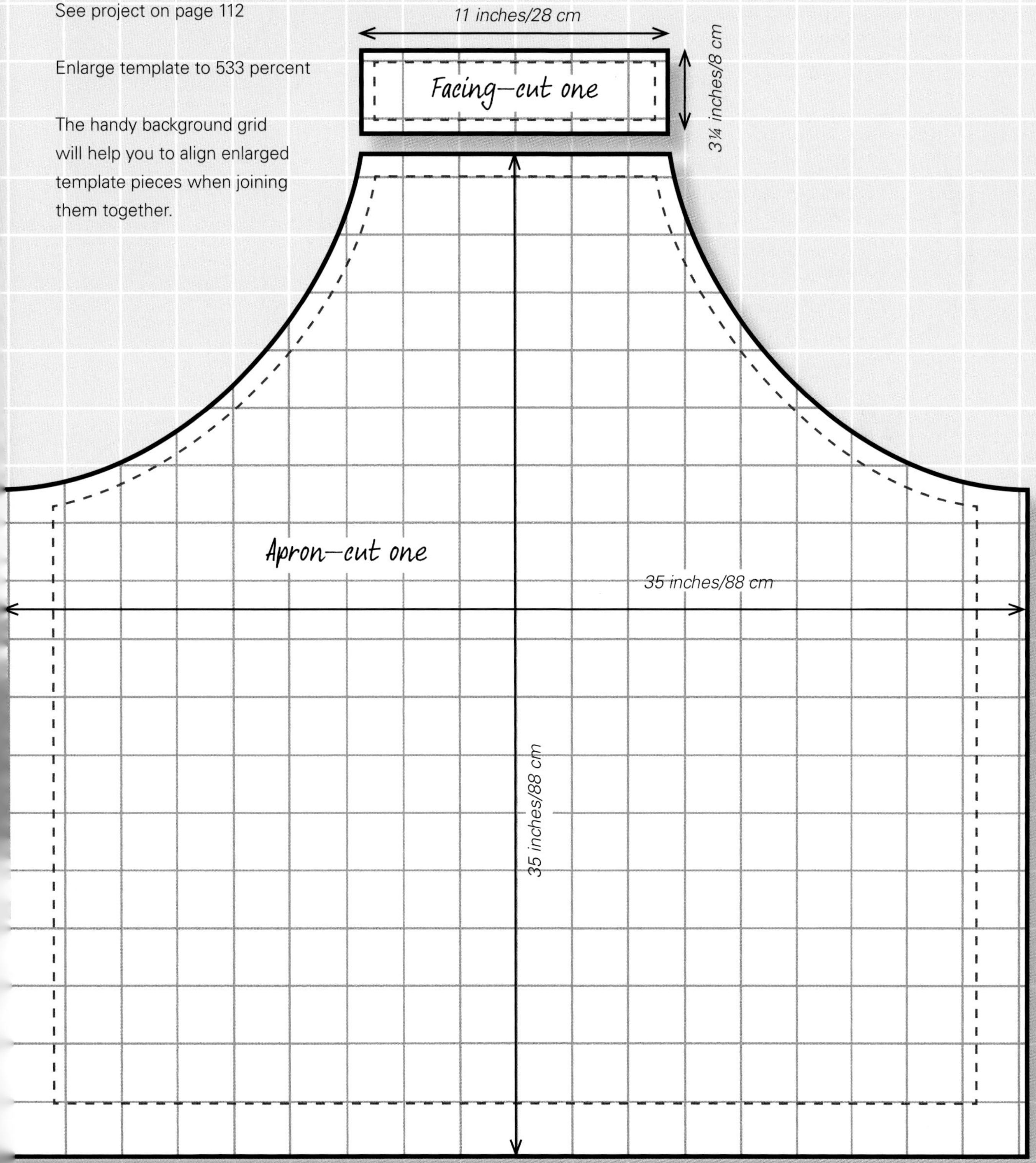

11 inches/28 cm

Facing—cut one

3¼ inches/8 cm

Apron—cut one

35 inches/88 cm

35 inches/88 cm

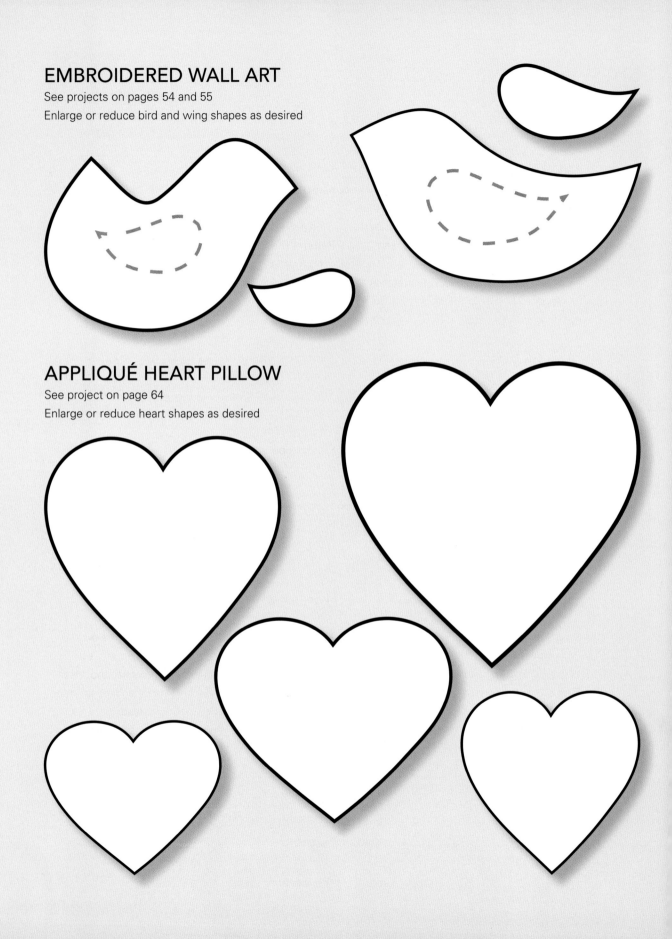

EMBROIDERED WALL ART

See projects on pages 54 and 55

Enlarge or reduce bird and wing shapes as desired

APPLIQUÉ HEART PILLOW

See project on page 64

Enlarge or reduce heart shapes as desired

GLOSSARY

Appliqué Sewing a piece of fabric on top of another. This can be done by machine, using a tight zigzag stitch, or by hand using a blind stitch.

Basting A temporary long running stitch made to hold fabric pieces together; the stitches are removed after final stitching.

Batting Fiberfill, cotton, wool, or other stuffing material that is flattened and comes on a roll and bought by the yard/meter. Used to fill placemats, quilts, and other home furnishing projects.

Bias Any diagonal direction of a fabric. The stretch is in the bias direction. True bias is the diagonal edge formed when a fabric is folded so that the lengthwise and crosswise grains are aligned. True bias has a 45-degree angle. Woven fabrics have the greatest amount of stretch along the true bias.

Bias binding A finishing trim that is made from fabric strips cut along the bias grain. Fabric cut on this grain has a great deal of stretch, so that the tape fits around curves without puckering. It can be made to match or bought ready made.

Bobbin The small metal spool of thread that feeds the bottom thread through on a sewing machine. *See also Spool.*

Edge stitching An extra row of stitching on the very edge of a garment, usually 1/8 inch/3 mm or less from a seam line, fold line, or finished edge. The thread color usually matches the fabric.

Fat quarter Used mostly for patchwork or quilting. A ¼ yard or meter of fabric, cut by dividing one yard/meter in half both horizontally and vertically, so that you get four pieces ready cut measuring roughly 22 x 18 inches/57 x 50 cm (as opposed to a regular ¼ yard or meter, which is 9 x 45 inches/25 x 115 cm).

Grain The direction of the threads in woven fabrics. Crosswise grain: from left to right. Straight grain: from top to bottom, parallel with the selvages.

Interfacing Fabrics used to support, reinforce, and give shape to fashion fabrics placed in between the lining and the outer fabric. Some interfacings are fusible (sticking when heat pressed using an iron), others are stitched in place.

Knit fabric A fabric produced from a single end of yarn held together by looping the yarns around each other, creating ridges of different depths depending on the thickness of the thread. Jersey, T-shirt fabric, and fleece are all examples of knit fabrics.

Nap A texture on fabric that runs in only one direction—for example, the pile on velvet or the ridges on corduroy.

Pattern The pattern is the paper or cardstock template from which the project pieces are copied onto a fabric before being cut out and stitched together.

Raw edge The unstitched or nonfinished edge of fabric.

Running stitch The simplest sewing stitch made by running the thread under and over the fabric.

Seam The line where two pieces of fabric are held together by a line of stitching.

Seam allowance The distance between the cut edge of the fabric and the line stitched along when joining two or more pieces of fabric together.

Seam ripper A small tool used for removing stitches.

Selvage The term used to describe the self-finished edges of fabric when woven. The selvages prevent the fabric from raveling or fraying on the side edges.

Shirring Sewing across a fabric with thin, tubular elastic thread, which then pulls the fabric in. The bobbin is wound with shirring elastic and the top thread is normal sewing thread.

Spool A tube or cone used to hold sewing thread; *see also Bobbin.*

Topstitching An extra row of stitching on the outside of a garment along or near a finished edge, usually as a decorative finish but often functional, too. Used on patch pockets, straps, belts, and handles, it can be worked in a matching or contrast thread.

Warp The set of lengthwise threads that are held in tension on any form of loom, from domestic to industrial, and are the foundation of all woven fabrics.

Weft The crosswise threads inserted over and under the warp threads in woven fabrics.

Woven fabric A fabric produced on a loom by weaving crosswise threads over and under lengthwise threads. Cotton and linen are woven fabrics.

INDEX